6200092

ELLSWORTH
—on—
ELLSWORTH

An unchronological, mostly
true account of some
moments of contact
between "library science"
and me, since our
confluence in 1931, with
appropriate sidelights.

RALPH E. ELLSWORTH

The Scarecrow Press, Inc.
Metuchen, N.J.,
and London, 1980.

Library of Congress Cataloging in Publication Data

Ellsworth, Ralph Eugene, 1907-
    Ellsworth on Ellsworth.

        Bibliography: p.
        Includes index.
        1.   Ellsworth, Ralph Eugene, 1907-
2.   Librarians--United States--Biography.
3.   Library science.   I.   Title.
    Z720. E65A34   020'. 92'4   80-12656
    ISBN 0-8108-1311-4

To Theda, always an equal partner

TABLE OF CONTENTS

Preface   vii
1931--The Year Library Science and I Discovered
    Each Other   1
        My First Experience as a Librarian   7
Early Years in Iowa, Including Some of the Habits
    of Farm Animals   11
        What a Young Boy Did on an Iowa Farm in
            the "Olden Days"   16
        The Livestock Economy   20
Off to College   23
Library School   28
        The Waples-Thompson Arguments   29
My Experiences at the Graduate Library School,
    University of Chicago, 1934-37   32
Seven Years at the University of Colorado, 1937-44   40
Another Chance at Modular Planning at Iowa   47
Projects I Was Involved with at Iowa, 1944-58   51
        The Midwest Inter-Library Center (Now Center
            for Research Libraries)   51
        The Cooperative Committee on Large University
            Library Building Planning   56
        The Dissertation Abstracts Project   58
        Centralized Cataloging   61
        The American Right Wing Collection Project   74
        The American Library Association 75th
            Anniversary Celebration and the American
            Heritage Program of Adult Education   78
        How I Almost Played Poker with President
            Harry S Truman   80
I Return to Colorado   84
        Conducting Seminars on Building Planning   86
        The School Library Book   88
Visiting and Consulting with Foreign Libraries   91
        Sweden. Stockholm University   93
        Iran. The Pahlavi Imperial Library and
            Center   95
        Saudi Arabia. Riyadh University   99

Venezuela.   Simon Bolivar University   104
Yugoslavia.   Titograd University   106
Several Libraries in Mexico   110
My Sabbatical Year Project 1969-70   114
Consulting Work in the United States   115
Things that Shouldn't Happen to a Consultant   116
The University of Pittsburgh Consultation   117
Wyoming.   The University of Wyoming   118
California State College   119
Wells College, Aurora, New York   119
Oberlin, Ohio   120
Mount St. Scholastica, Atchison, Kansas   121
Associating with Library Associations   122
American Library Association   123
Association of Research Libraries   129
And More...   130
Publications Since 1958   134
The Colorado Academic Central Processing
Project   136
A Matter of Style   136
Retirement   138
Physical Ineptitudes   140
Some Extras--Fishing and the Cabin   142
Conclusion   150
References Cited   153
Index

PREFACE

Well, if H. Faulkner Brown could get away with the subtitle "Metcalf and Ellsworth at York" for his York seminar book, and if my good friend and colleague, Ellsworth Mason, can call his new book Mason on Library Buildings, then I feel justified in using the title I have chosen. After all, as Asimov said in a recent television interview, "I am my favorite subject." And shouldn't a book title reflect, as well as predict, the contents of the book it heads?

When I use the term Library Science, I refer not to the usage at the time of Melvil Dewey, but to its usage at the time of the Waples-Thompson exchange of charges in 1931.

This is not a normal autobiography. If it were I should have had to write about myself and my family and the social milieu in which I have lived. And, lest I cheat my readers out of some choice morsel, I should have had to wait until nearer the end. Instead, the book is an attempt to comment on the ways of the library profession in response to the infusion of a new concept--the scientific spirit--as introduced by the University of Chicago Graduate Library School in the early 1930s. I have also tucked in a few unassuming comments on the behavior of some of my colleagues during this period.

And, like a properly conducted funeral, the account attempts to cover the subject but not be too darned serious about it.

Alas, I find that I have, in spite of good intentions, slipped onto the stage too often, stealing the lines from the narrative. For this I apologize. The flesh has been strong but the spirit has been weak!

I have tried to remember that no person should attempt to evaluate the impact of his efforts on events, but that it is fair for him to state what he thinks he has done, especially if he can supply documentation. Usually, the future can be relied upon to correct distortions. And if not, the reviewers can.

I wish to thank those who have helped edit the manuscript: my wife, Theda; Anne Walton; Ann Dougherty and Bernita Ellsworth. Anne Walton deserves special thanks for typing two editions of the manuscript.

1931--THE YEAR LIBRARY SCIENCE
AND I DISCOVERED EACH OTHER

1931 was the year President Herbert Hoover told us that prosperity was just around the corner. It wasn't! For librarians, 1931 introduced a new concept of Library Science through the Waples-Thompson debates in Library Journal on the research work of Waples and others at the University of Chicago Graduate Library School. 1931 was also the year I entered the profession as Librarian of Adams State College in Alamosa, Colorado.

The June 1931 Western Reserve University School of Library Science graduating class, consisting of three males and some one hundred and twenty females, faced a bleak job market. By July, few of the graduates had found jobs and my hopes of getting married were sinking lower and lower. Then suddenly, on a gloomy, rainy August day in Cleveland, came an offer of the job of Librarian from the President of Adams State College at $2,000.00 a year if I were married. I wired immediately that I wasn't but would be if the salary would support a wife. The President then raised the ante to $2,250.00 and I accepted, but not until I had pacified my wife-to-be, Theda, who wasn't too happy at being valued at $250.00 per year--her services, that is. The $2,250.00 salary was, by the way, the largest received by any Western Reserve Library School 1931 graduate.

Early in September my bride and I took off for the West on the New York Central, riding in a day coach attached to a mail train, with a luncheon basket properly filled with fried chicken and other things appropriate to the occasion. After a few hours spent in Chicago visiting with my college roommate, we boarded the Rock Island for an overnight ride to Des Moines. I had no contact with the Adams State College, only the exchange of telegrams, and this worried me some, especially since the college seemed not to have made the directories as yet.

A one-day stopover in Des Moines with my parents

gave me an opportunity to hunt up my old White Powder
Wonder shot gun (Montgomery Ward) that my brother and I
had used on Iowa rabbits, squirrels and pheasants during our
early years.   Much to the embarrassment of Theda (a city
girl), I squeezed the gun stock into my suitcase, but the barrel I had to strap on the outside, sticking out several inches
at both ends.

Our first real marital problem arose when the two of
us--both tall--tried to figure out how to dress and undress in
a lower Pullman berth with two suitcases, one of which had
a long shot gun barrel strapped to the outside.   I no longer
remember the details, but the problem got solved, with
sound effects that must have been quite disturbing to the se-
date lady in the upper berth above us.   I did notice that the
next morning at breakfast in the diner she carefully averted
her eyes and avoided sitting across the table from us.

In the morning cinders and soot from the coal-fired
engine that pulled our train covered our pillows.   We had to
have the window open lest we suffocate, since there was no
air conditioning in 1931.   However, a big breakfast of wheat
cakes and sausage and pots of coffee, all served on a white,
linen-covered table with cloth napkins by a cheerful waiter,
revived us as we watched an empty Kansas landscape roll by.
Anyone on that train who couldn't see the wagon trains and
hostile Indians waiting to pounce on the pioneers from behind the rolling hills was sadly lacking in imagination.

The conductor quickly spotted us as Eastern (Ohio)
newlyweds, and he devoted his spare time, of which he
seemed to have quite a lot, introducing us to the West--real
and fancy.   Somehow his best stories centered around the
remarkable capability of the clean mountain air to shorten
distances for newcomers, and to cause tourists who thought
they were jumping over a mere brook to fall into streams,
and hikers to spend days approaching a mountain that appeared to be only a mile or so away.   I doubt if he told us
anything really useful, but it shortened his day, and amused
us.   We had trouble seeing our first prairie dog because we
kept looking for an animal the size of the German shepherd
we had left with family in Ohio.   We saw no antelope, nor
buffalo, and very few cattle--just empty rolling hills and a
few small towns in between.

Since our train arrived in Colorado Springs after dark
the second day out, we still had not seen a mountain when we

went to bed, but the next morning, after a night in the old
Alamo hotel (where my wife's parents had stayed thirty years
earlier), there was Pike's Peak--our first mountain--covered
with fresh snow and very, very big and high.

Later that day we boarded a Rio Grande and Western
train for Salida via the Royal Gorge and entered a packed
coach, with my shot gun barrel causing no end of trouble as
I tried to fit my suitcase in the rack above our heads, only
to be told it couldn't stay there but would have to be left in
the vestibule, where it got in the way of everybody passing
by. As I recall, there were a few "I told you so" comments
passed in my direction. From Salida, we proceeded to Alamosa on a bus with much freight and mail and only three
passengers--the two of us and the Supervisor of Nursing at
the Alamosa hospital. She was gentle and amusing and she
gave us much useful information about living in the San Luis
Valley, including the possibility of being able to play tennis
all winter. She taught us how to pronounce some of the
Spanish town names. For instance, one didn't pronounce La
Jara so it sounded like jar. Nor did one pronounce Saguache
to sound like gauche.

As we came down off the south side of Poncha Pass,
we entered the Valley at the north end, and what a sight!
The San Luis Valley (about sixty by one hundred twenty miles
in size) was bordered on the east by the rugged and snow-
covered Sangre de Cristo Range, and on the west by the older,
tree-covered San Juan Range. The floor of the valley seemed
flat and was covered by cactus, sage, rabbit brush, and a few
cottonwood trees along the stream beds. Occasionally a jack
rabbit took off from under bushes near the road, but he
hopped only far enough to be out of danger from the bus.
Artesian wells were everywhere, pumping water into irrigation ditches, which made possible the growing of potatoes,
peas, lettuce and hay fields--all new to us. But the cultivated
land seemed to be only a very small part of the vista. The
rest was wild, vast and silent.

We saw in the distance the famous Sand Dunes, and
we watched the sunset turn the Sangre de Cristos into a deep
pink color--a thrilling sight to flatlanders, or to anyone who
had eyes with a feeling for beauty.

The hotel clerk, when we checked in in Alamosa, remarked that he too was an Easterner (from Ohio), and we
began to sense that geography was relative. After dinner I

called the President of the College, ostensibly to announce
our arrival, but really to reassure myself that I really did
have a job and that Adams State really existed. (It wasn't
mentioned in some of the directories I had consulted.)

We shook the dust off our clothes and ourselves and
went to bed bathless, the hotel plumbing being out of order.
After breakfast we went outside to case the joint and to find
the college. We saw no buildings that looked like a college,
but after walking along the main street we saw a large building and my hopes rose; but alas, that was the city high
school. Finally all by itself, on the edge of town stood a
Colonial-type structure, with one wing attached and one wing
missing. Above the front door was a sign, "Adams State
Normal School." That was it. The campus consisted of
sand, cactus, rabbit brush and sage. There was a patch of
green grass along the sidewalk and drive up to the front of
the building. Around the periphery of the campus was a
hedge of small Russian olive trees, fed by an irrigation ditch.
And one could see irrigated areas which had been cleared and
planted with grass. There were two tennis courts visible.

We presented ourselves to the President, a most gracious and friendly man who first showed us the library. It
consisted of one large reading room, two small office and
work rooms, and a two-level bookstack, holding about 5,500
books.

The President then walked us to the apartment building nearby where we were to live. He, by the way, had
built these apartments out of his own pocket, as a means of
housing the faculty (about twenty-five), although two or three
lived in their own houses or in apartments elsewhere in town.
One didn't have to live in the Casa del Sol apartments, but
if there were vacancies some pressure was put on those who
didn't live there. The apartment consisted of a living room
and kitchen, a heated dressing room and bath and an unheated
bedroom. It was built on the very edge of town and an un-
fenced desert started right outside our bedroom window.

For weeks our furniture consisted of a bed and a big
packing case, which contained our lares and penates shipped
earlier from Ohio, and finally a large lounge chair we were
able to purchase. We could cook, sleep, sit together
in the big chair, and read. What more does a young
happy couple need? We ordered furniture, but in 1931
furniture manufacturers were going broke right and left and

orders went unfilled. It was months before we were able to
get a day bed, dining table and chairs. Someone loaned us
a card table in the meanwhile, and the kitchen had a built-in
table. My wife crocheted a large rug out of strips of cloth
she had brought along, bought and begged from neighbors.

Since my White Powder Wonder shot gun hadn't been
fired for many years I wasn't sure how safe it was. So we
took it out into the desert near the Rio Grande River--which
flowed less than a half mile from the apartment--propped it
up against an irrigation ditch bank, tied a string to the trigger, crouched behind the ditch bank and pulled the trigger.
It made a big noise and jumped into the air, but it didn't ex-
plode and I felt vindicated for bringing it all the way from
Des Moines strapped to the outside of my suitcase. I didn't
ask my wife what she thought. I had visions of stocking our
larder with rabbits, ducks and other edible fauna. We didn't
actually have a larder big enough to hold a rabbit, because
refrigerators in those days had very small freezer compart-
ments, but then the few rabbits (cottontails) I managed to
shoot we ate right away. And the only duck I managed to
capture I found caught in a trap along the banks of the Rio
Grande and we ate it immediately.

Our first Thanksgiving in Alamosa came close to being
my last. The afternoon before Thanksgiving I went hunting
down by the Rio Grande. Thinking the rabbits on the other
side would be more numerous, I waded across. I found none
on that side either. But when I started to wade back I discovered an upstream irrigation dam had been opened, raising
the level of the water by a foot or so; I nearly drowned getting back. And while I was struggling across, a blizzard
suddenly hit. The wind blew the snow violently in all directions and visibility was zero. I was wet and cold and plenty
scared. I was afraid to leave the river for fear of getting
lost in the open desert between the river and our apartment--
not more than a half mile. Had I not run into the remnants
of a fence, along which I could crawl back to town, I would
never have made it.

That storm lasted for days and was followed by so
much more snow and cold weather that the snow never left
the ground until the next May. Needless to say, there was
no tennis in Alamosa that winter.

Being young and healthy, each night we opened the
windows in our bedroom wide, even though one night it went

to 38° below zero in the room. Mounds of ice piled upon the blankets near our mouths. One morning when we awakened there was a burro's head in the window gazing solemnly at us. Perhaps he was wondering why we were so foolish as to leave our window open. Fortunately he resisted the temptation to bray.

That winter, 1931, set all kinds of records for low temperatures. During the month of January the temperature never got up to zero. The weekly laundry, which Theda had to do in two soap-stone tubs without benefit of a powered washing machine or a wringer, had to be hung up on lines located on the roof of the communal garage. In the cold weather the laundry froze the minute it was hung up, and when the strong winds whipped it around, handling a bed sheet became a dangerous operation. Theda's respect for the pioneer women increased. So did her muscles. If people went to town to see a movie, the women put newspapers inside their stockings to keep their legs from freezing. Women didn't wear slacks in those days.

The first year we had no car, but our friends, the Tingles, the high school music teacher and his wife, owned a Chevrolet roadster with side curtains but no heater. Skiing on $2.97 Montgomery Ward skis with leather toe straps with the Tingles was great while the sun was out, but the thrity-mile drive home after dark in -20° weather was cold even though four of us were pretty closely packed in the Chevy. It took bowls of chili and bottles of home brewed beer to thaw us out.

In 1931, the poor people in Alamosa were close to starving. Hunters donated jackrabbits and other game they didn't want to eat themselves. One -20° Saturday morning Tingle and I went out to shoot our share. Each time we would manage to hit a jackrabbit it would jump three feet into the air, and before it landed it was usually frozen stiff. The starving Spanish people were glad to get the rabbits. I attempted one once, but never got beyond the skinning stage. Too gamy for me.

In February '32 we bought a secondhand Ford roadster for $125.00 (without a heater, of course) and this freed us for picnics, fishing, skiing expeditions and other trips.

Near Alamosa at Hooper there was a hot water spring, with a primitive swimming pool surrounded by a six-foot

wooden fence to keep the steam from the water contained so
that one could swim there in the winter time.   The water
was 107° as it entered the pool.   Undressing in unheated
dressing rooms was torture, but once in the pool a good soak
warmed one up sufficiently so that going outside and rolling
in the snow was possible.   Personally, we never tried that.
A favorite treatment for visiting friends was to take them for
a hamburger fry at the Sand Dunes, and then after dark sug-
gest that we go swimming.   They usually protested, but we
insisted.   After the shock of the dressing rooms passed and
they lay on their backs in hot water gazing up at the stars
and snow-capped mountains, they really enjoyed it.   No one
ever seemed to catch cold from the experience.

My First Experience as a Librarian

As I said earlier, there were fewer than 6,000 books in the
library at Adams State, and my first year we had a book fund
of less than $100.00.   The College boasted of one special
collection, consisting of a hundred or so out-of-date medical
books donated from the estate of a local doctor.

Since I was the only librarian, I found myself doing
everything from opening the library at 7:30 a.m. to closing
it at 5 p.m.   I cataloged what few books we acquired, worked
at the circulation desk, answered a few reference questions
and supervised a small staff of student assistants.

Louise Kampf, Librarian at Colorado College, told me
they were terribly cramped for space and that I could have
for Adams State an entire attic full of unbound volumes of
19th-century general magazines.   So we took them--three
truckloads.   I climbed up in the attic, which was boiling hot,
and tossed the volumes to a student assistant who loaded them
in the truck.   In order to make these magazines more available, I organized a simple bindery, using an electric drill
for piercing and sewing, cakes of animal hoof glue, muslin,
mill ends of buckram and stiff card boards for covers.   We
trained students to do the work at 25¢ per hour, and not only
put several through college with their earnings, but made the
magazines available at a very low cost.   The results weren't
fancy, but they were adequate.   We later branched out and
re-bound text books for nearby schools, at a very low cost--
10¢ per volume, as I remember.   The smell of melting cakes
of hoof glue permeated the entire building and competed suc-

cessfully, if not pleasingly, with the smells from the Chemistry Department. The President told me there was no money for book shelves, so I collected apple and orange crates for the shelves. These worked but they looked so shoddy that the President soon found money for decent shelving.

Most of the faculty were able to accumulate very little cash, and we didn't carry much with us. Consequently, when President Roosevelt closed the banks in 1932, many of us were in need of cash. Fortunately, food costs were low. For example, potatoes cost 50¢ per hundred pounds, coffee 17¢ a pound, Texas grapefruit--delivered to your door--cost 50¢ a bushel, and our monthly grocery bill, excluding milk, seldom ran over $17.00. Our butcher let us have meat on credit during the entire bank holiday. Also, I had written a check to Oberlin College, as a payment on my postponed tuition bill, and it was in the mail during the holiday. Oberlin waited patiently.

We entertained ourselves by reading, visiting with friends, playing a little bridge, skiing in the winter, fishing in the summer and exploring the fabulous country the year around, including trips to Sante Fe and the Indian country. The faculty held a monthly supper and bridge party which was a pain in the neck, but everyone had to go.

My wife, who played the cello, was drafted by the Chamber of Commerce to go on "booster" trips as part of a string trio to play at nearby towns to promote trade in Alamosa. One of these, Sanford, had a high school gym floor mounted on coil springs so that when one danced the whole floor swayed and jumped. This being a Mormon community, coffee was not served. However, there was plenty of cocoa, the Mormons not knowing, apparently, that cocoa has more caffeine than does coffee. One met all kinds of people at these sociables, and a fascinating community of people they were. We thoroughly enjoyed ourselves.

By virtue of the smallness of the College, every faculty member served on several all-College committees, and I quickly developed the habit of thinking about problems on a college-wide basis--a privilege which seemed very important to me. And we took on extra duties without grousing too much. For example, one summer session, in addition to running the library, in my spare time I taught introductory courses in Political Science, Sociology and Economics. I had learned enough at Oberlin to handle most of these courses,

but when it came to the section on insurance in the Economics
course I had to tell the students that I couldn't understand insurance and they would have to learn about it from someone
else. Thank goodness this was in the pre-Keynesian days!

My lifelong habit of writing articles for periodicals
had its beginning in the early Alamosa days, although the im-
petus probably came from a conversation the previous year
with George F. Strong, a fine, sensitive gentlemen who was
Librarian of Adelbert College, Western Reserve University
at the time I worked as a student assistant while studying
for my B. S. in L. S. One day while talking with me about
an annotated bibliography on Soviet Russia I had written, he
told me that I should try to write and publish when I became
a librarian. I took his advice seriously as soon as I could.
One of my duties as Librarian at Adams State was to catalog
newly acquired phonograph records. I found no help in the
library literature and so I wrote an article on the subject,
which to my surprise the Library Journal published. Also,
School and Society published a short article I wrote on Teachers Colleges and school libraries. These two experiences
gave me a taste of blood, which I have tried to satisfy all
my life, much to the chagrin of young librarians who have
had to read the stuff and to reviewers who haven't liked what
I have written.

A second lucky break happened at one of the Colorado
Library Association sessions in 1933. Mr. C. H. Smith,
then Librarian at the University of Colorado, was snoozing
while serving as a member of a panel. Somebody asked him
a question and he was having difficulty in handling the situation. I broke in and distracted the discussion until C. Henry
could become fully awake. He was grateful and later helped
me become his successor in 1936.

The sessions of the Colorado Library Association were
usually held in Denver so that we provincial librarians could
do some shopping in the big city and enjoy the benefits of
civilization. Naturally, I attended them. I soon became acquainted with Dean Harriet Howe of the University of Denver
School of Librarianship. She, having just come to the deanship from the faculty of the University of Chicago Graduate
Library School, was apparently watching for recruits for G.
L. S. She urged me to think about going there for a Ph. D.,
and I became interested and did apply for admission and a
fellowship in 1934. I feel pretty certain that her backing was

a major factor in my winning a university fellowship at G. L. S. for the fall of 1934.

But before I get serious about the early days of "Library Science" and me, I had better depart from my good intentions and do a little autobiographical sketching, not because the account is of any importance but because it interests me, and may interest my readers, if any.

EARLY YEARS IN IOWA,
including some of the habits of farm animals

I was delivered by a homeopathic doctor in a log cabin house on a farm west of Forest City, Iowa, on September 22, 1907. The date is important because, as readers of horoscopes (of which I am not one) know, those who were born on that date have split personalities, between Virgos and Libras: shall one dash out seizing every opportunity in sight as a Virgo, or flop on the bed pulling the covers over one's head to avoid disasters, as a Libra?

Earliest recollections:

Being brokenhearted after accidentally killing a wren with a sling shot.

Riding to church in a surrey (yes, with a fringe on top) behind frisky horses.

Being driven to a one-room school on stormy winter mornings in a horse-drawn sleigh, covered with a heavy buffalo robe.

Saturday afternoon shopping trips to town--Tom Mix movies, dinner with grandparents, asking my grandfather how many rebels he had killed in the Civil War and never finding out.

The smell of coffee being ground in my uncle's general store while neighbors visited in German, Swedish, Norwegian and Danish, and listening with amazement at my uncle's ability to talk to all of them. Clerks dashing around filling big cartons from long shopping lists. Spending pennies at the candy counter for small glass tubes of pinhead-sized candies. New yellow, button shoes with hard toes.

Sleeping in upstairs unheated bedrooms on corn husk mattresses, with newspapers between the blankets to keep us warm.

Repeated soakings in tubs of hot water, followed by massages
by my grandmother to cure my case of polio when I was
two years old.

My father test-driving a Model T Ford, and crashing into a
barn while he pulled one way on the steering wheel and
the salesman the other.

Backing a buggy into a lake and fishing for bullheads from
the buggy, and filling the tub with them.

German neighbors arguing among themselves over Germany's
World War I policies.

Furnishing boy power to run the washing machine into which
Mother lifted, with a broom stick, clothes that had been
boiling in a long copper tub on the kitchen wood stove.

Riding ten miles in a bobsled filled with straw, covered with
the buffalo robe, to spend a Christmas weekend with relatives.

Suffering from hard belly aches from eating green apples in
spite of warnings from my parents.

Being given a taste of home brewed beer at Swedish great
uncle's home.

Deliberately cutting my hand on a cabbage slicer so that I
could go out and play ball instead of helping to make sau-
erkraut. (It didn't work! My mother saw through the
scheme.)

I have since wondered how it happened that I, a male
WASP with all those privileges, didn't rise to the Presidency
--not even the presidency of a university or of A. L. A. The
only reason I can give is that by the time of my birth, the
log cabin had been covered with white clapboards.

I remember at an early age discussing the possibilities
with my mother: "Mother, what shall I do to become President of the United States, or a University President, or at
least a Dean? I don't want to have to settle for being a mere
Librarian. "

"Well, son, " she said, "the first thing to do is join
the right political party. Probably it's best to become a mod-

erate Republican. Then get yourself appointed to as many
university committees as possible, especially those that never
do much; cultivate a mellifluous, soothing speaking voice and
offer wise compromises in faculty debates. Back the athletic
program to the hilt, and attend all football games. Volunteer
for community service committees--the easiest ones to get on
are the ones that raise money for hearts, livers, and kidney
transplants. Finally, you may get to head up the United Way
drive, and then you will know that you have arrived. Of
course, join the Chamber of Commerce. When the Call comes,
accept membership in Rotary, Kiwanis or Lions--in that order of preference.

"Don't take long summer vacations. Sort of drop
around the president's office and let it be known that you are
available to help out if any special crisis arises.

"Be patient. Work your way up by accepting small
assignments on committees but be careful to keep enlarging
your responsibilities. But be warned about one thing. If
you should become too distinguished for your own research,
and begin to win many awards, people will say, 'Yes, he'd
make a good president but we have so few outstanding re-
searchers we just can't spare him for administrative work.'
You'll just have to choose."

I thought long and hard about her advice, and I have
learned that it is sound if you want to become a university
president or a dean. But for a librarian's position you don't
have to do any of those things, thank God!

Before Iowa farms became highly mechanized in the
1920s much work was done by itinerant farm hands, men who
came and went from farm to farm, as they pleased. I learned
much from them, including every swear word that existed and
many off-color stories. They taught me to use Copenhagen
snuff and to chew Red Star tobacco. One of them once told
me that if I would put an empty clay jug in the bottom of the
silo before it was filled with silage, by next summer, when
the silo was emptied again, the jug would be filled with fine
whiskey. I did put the jug in the silo, but we moved away
before the next summer and I never found out if it was full
of whiskey. Come to think of it, I didn't even know what
whiskey was, even though I had tasted beer.

My first three years of schooling were spent in a one-
room school located on a corner of our farm near Forest City.

At the end of that year we moved to another farm near Gold-field, Iowa, where my father ran a purebred livestock farm--Hereford cattle, Poland China hogs, White Wyandotte chickens, Percheron horses and assorted sheep, ducks and geese. I raised greyhounds.

Although we raised enough corn, hay and oats to feed the animals and maybe sell the surplus, if any, the emphasis was on the animals. I had the good fortune to do all the kinds of work that are done on such a farm, and to operate the machinery that is involved. I also milked cows. Getting up before dawn and dressing in a cold bedroom on a winter morning in Iowa, tramping through the snow to the barn and then squatting down precariously on a one-peg milk stool and tucking your head into that nice warm hollow just above a cow's milk bag and first squirting milk into the mouths of the row of cats that always gathered for the occasion was an experience that is supposed to make Herbert Hoovers out of boys. As they wander around in the yards, cows collect small mud balls at the ends of the hair on their tails. Then as you sit there peacefully milking her, the cow loves to switch her tail and zapp you on the side of the head with those mud balls. This not only disturbs your serenity but it hurts like hell. My incurable habit of resorting to profanity (which I had learned from the hired hands) when startled had its origin from the zapping of the cow's tails. And then, just when you had recovered your aplomb, the old gal loved to kick your milk pail, spilling the contents on the ground, thus causing you to lose your temper again. Many a milker after such treatment returned the compliment by kicking the cow.

Although I don't expect anyone to believe me, I firmly believe that the things I learned while watching the behavior of animals on a livestock farm has increased my understanding of the rational and irrational behavior of people--especially academic people, including librarians. Which reminds me of the comment made to me by the Dean of the Liberal Arts College of one of the Big Ten universities, that far too much of his time had to be spent with faculty members who either failed to pay their rent or tried to seduce the wives of their colleagues.

At any rate, as a child I was fascinated by the behavior of the animals. Animals seemed to have just two things in mind: food and sex (or breeding, as we called it. I didn't learn the word sex until much later). That's what it was all about, morning, noon and night. I couldn't help wondering why female animals tolerated sex only when in heat a few days each year, whereas human females don't ordinarily tolerate sex when "in heat," but just about any other time they are in the mood. But what were those male animals, who were ready for sex every hour of every day, supposed to do while they were waiting for the females to be ready, once a year? Did this affect their psyches and make them neurotic, as it is supposed to for human males? And then I wondered why it was that the female animal's external sex organs were pretty much alike except in size, whereas the male sex organs differed widely, from the post-like organ of the horse, to the twice-as-long organ of a burro (who was less than half as big as a horse), to the slender corkscrew penis of a hog. And why was it that the horse, of all the farm animals, was the only one that raised holy hell before and during the sex act--snorting, biting and kicking? Maybe because the sex act was difficult for him and so he had to hype himself up to be able to perform.

And why did a wild duck try to hold his mate's head under water while he bred her? And why, of all the farm animals, was the male dog so constructed that after his orgasm he had to wait five or ten minutes before the nodules on his penis contracted enough so he could withdraw? One of the most pathetic sights one saw among breeding animals was to watch two dogs standing at right angles to each other, waiting for things to subside. Apparently this physiological situation is common among all dogs, for I noticed recently that above the finish line of the annual dog sled race from Anchorage to Nome, Alaska, there hangs, most appropriately, a huge phallic dog penis carved from a tree trunk, with its nodules plainly visible.

And why was it that the female animals showed neither pleasure nor displeasure during the sex act, whereas all male animals acted as though they enjoyed it? And how come that of all the males on the farm, only the rooster stood up and told the world of his conquest? All the other animals simply resumed eating.

I have never found any answers to these questions, but I have thought that it would be nice if someone like Freud would make a study of the situation.

What a Young Boy Did on an
Iowa Farm in the "Olden Days"

For me, living on an Iowa farm in the pre-mechanized days
was 80% fun and 20% work.   Long summer days were spent
swimming in the muddy Boone River, and in the spring time
swimming over the town dam--a forbidden, as well as dangerous, thing to do;   riding down the swollen river on float-
ing trees or other debris that happened along, and afterwards
getting a whipping for engaging in such forbidden sport;   raid-
ing the neighbor's gardens for muskmelons in the fall and his
trees for walnuts;   hunting squirrels, rabbits, and pheasants;
fishing for bullheads, carp and suckers;   and in the fall and
winters trapping for muskrats, mink and skunks, in hopes of
being able to sell the furs for money with which to buy boys'
gear--hopes which were never realized.   No one ever seemed
to want to buy the furs.

The Old Settlers' Day picnic and Fourth of July cele-
brations in the city park, where everyone gathered, were oc-
casions for listening to long-winded speeches by local orators
and stuffing oneself at the picnic tables loaded with all kinds
of food--fried chicken, potato salad, etc.   Likewise the Chau-
tauqua week, when the family tent was pitched in the park and
everyone listened to orchestras, bell concerts, over-age opera
singers, and once even William Jennings Bryan.

And in the wintertime we skied on homemade skis, the
tips of which we bent by soaking boards in tall cans into which
steam was introduced from the mechanism used to heat the
animals' food in freezing weather.   Northern Iowa is flat but
around Goldfield there were many hills just right for sledding
and skiing.   And after the river froze there was skating (always an adventure because of the air pockets where the river
currents were strong.   After a dunking in that cold water the
mile home tramp in freezing clothes wasn't exactly fun).   We
also cut holes in the ice and speared huge carp and catfish
as they passed under the holes.

The big barns all had a second level into which loose
and baled hay would be piled in the late summer.   The bales
made marvelous building blocks with which to construct cas-
tles with runways into which girls could be enticed for what
we thought was necking.   Usually by midwinter the hay would
have been used up to such an extent that the floor could be
used for a basket-ball court.   On Sundays after church the
neighborhood boys would gather there for endless basketball

games. City boys weren't welcome because they insisted on smoking--which was absolutely forbidden in the haymow.

The 20% work included the daily chores such as cleaning out the manure from the horse and cattle barns and throwing down clean straw for the animals; feeding the animals with corn, hay and silage--which first had to be thrown down from the top of the silo (the level within the silo was lowered a little each day until spring, when it usually reached ground level); spreading corn and grain for the chickens; heating the hog food and then throwing it in troughs; gathering the eggs and picking up corn cobs to use in starting fires in the cook stove and furnace. The hired men did the heavier work and we boys did the minor tasks until we were big enough to do the heavy work, too. Then there was the seasonal work, such as loading the manure spreader and covering the fields in early spring before the ground thawed; spring plowing before planting corn and oats, and then at the right time planting both with special equipment. We planted pumpkin seeds in the corn hills, and then did the weekly plowing to keep the weeds down in the corn fields. At harvest time we picked up the oats bundles, which had been gathered and tied by machines, and stacked them into shocks for curing, after which the threshing began--a communal project.

The rig was owned by one farmer and he did each farmer's threshing in turn. Everybody followed the rig from farm to farm, and the women all helped feed the crew, which at times numbered fifty or so men and boys. Some of the oats were stored in bins in the barn, and the surplus was taken to the town grain elevator, where it was sold as a cash crop. The corn was husked late in the fall after the frosts had hardened the ears. The art of using a husker's peg to tear off the husks before throwing the corn ears into the wagon took some learning because it had to be done correctly. Otherwise, the husks, if left attached to the ears, would clog up the corn sheller. Each wagon was equipped with a side board on one side of the horse-drawn wagon so that the huskers wouldn't throw the ears clear over the wagon. The rhythmic bang, bang of the ears hitting the side board was a good sound to hear because from it one could tell how heavy the harvest was to be, and this was important to know because the livestock depended primarily on corn for their winter food.

Corn to be made into silage was gathered before the corn became entirely ripe. It had to be a bit moist so that

it would ferment. Big machines would go down the corn rows
cutting the corn stalks, which we gathered into bundles, tied
with twine and deposited on the ground. These bundles then
were gathered into shocks and, at the right time, brought to
the silos, where shredders cut up the shocks, usually with
the ears of corn on them, and blew them up a pipe into the
top of the silos, where they fermented and became cattle
feed. Silos were equipped with removable doors about two
feet square, which opened inward. These were inserted into
place as the level of the new silage rose and, conversely,
during the winter, were removed as the level fell. A covered chute built around these doors concentrated the silage
as, each day, enough would be thrown down for the animals.

I was allowed, at an early age, to drive the Model T
Ford truck from corn shock to corn shock and that's how I
learned to drive a car. Starting a Model T Ford in the winter was an art. First, one jacked up one rear wheel; then
one filled the radiator (which had been drained after the last
use) with hot water, pouring some on the manifold; then one
retarded the spark lever, pulled out the choke wire and began
to crank, always being sure one's thumb was on the same
side of the crank handle as the rest of the hand. Otherwise,
if the engine kicked back (which it usually did) one was likely
to get a broken arm or wrist. After much cranking the engine would usually start. One then leaped into the driver's
seat, pulled the spark lever down a bit, and then after the
engine was warm, moved the brake lever all the way forward,
pushed in the clutch pedal and away you went (provided someone had remembered to lower the rear wheel that had been
jacked up). The Model T Ford transmission mechanism was
marvelously complex and efficient, but very simple to operate,
all by foot.

At that time there were no paved, or even graveled,
roads in that part of Iowa and in the spring the mud roads
were nearly impassable for a car, but the Model Ts, which
had a high clearance and were very powerful in low gear,
frequently could get through where no other car could. Even
so it was quite common to have to bring out a team of horses
to pull the cars out of mud holes in the roads. Sometimes
the ruts would be a foot deep, and filled with water.

But to return to the work load of an Iowa boy. There
were special duties, too. As far as I know I am the only academic librarian in the U. S. A. with obstetrical experience. You
see, there was much money involved with raising pure bred

THE YANKEE 298,157

Poland China pigs around the 1920s. My father paid, for example, $40,000 for the Yankee, whose breeding fee was $500. Then when the Yankee died after four months of twice a day breeding, Orange Piece was purchased for $10,000.00. So, the maternity ward on the farm was important. It consisted of a long, low barn, with a caretaker's room (well heated and equipped with a cot) at one end and a series of farrowing pens the length of the barn. Sows about to give birth were put into these pens at the appropriate time. Mostly, the litters of piglets, ranging from five to eighteen in number, were born without difficulty; but now and then the process got stuck. Since I had slender hands and arms I would be drafted to assist in the delivery. One arm would be washed and covered with Vaseline clear to my shoulder. I would then reach into the sow's womb about a foot or so until I could get two fingers around a piglet's head and draw it out. This was painful for me (I assume it was for the sow, too) because her muscular contractions were powerful. It seems to me these sessions usually took place in the middle of the night, while I was sound asleep. The sows never seemed to protest against the assistance given them, perhaps because one soon learned how by means of tone of voice and manual pats and rubs to communicate with pigs, who in fact are very intelligent beasts and who respond quickly to people.

During the farrowing season someone stayed in the

caretaker's room twenty-four hours a day to take care of emergencies of various kinds.

The other animals may have had trouble with giving birth, but these had to be taken care of by the veterinarian, not by a ten-year-old boy.

The Livestock Economy

At least once a year the Poland China breeders would hold a sale at which they would sell to one another, and to new breeders, the offspring of their famous boars and sows. Catalogs with pictures, names and pedigrees of each animal to be sold would be printed, and mailed to other breeders. A large tent with tiered seats would be erected; lunch would be served to all who came; and buyers from out of town would be put up, free of charge, at the local hotels. An orchestra from nearby Clarion was hired to play while the crowd gathered and during lunch. My brother and I passed out cigars--some of which we pocketed and later smoked down by the river, where no one could see us. We agreed they were better than smoking grapevine stems or cornsilk wrapped in a sheet from the Sears Roebuck catalog, and I don't recall that they made us sick. But then, don't forget that we had chewed plug chewing tobacco, and Copenhagen snuff. We were tough.

Young sows bred to the Yankee or Orange Piece brought from $380.00 to $1,200.00 and some of the young boars that showed great promise went much higher. Everyone involved knew what characteristics in the hogs they were trying to breed to, and it was not difficult to see in a young hog what its future would be.

But suddenly, in common with all elements of the economy, the pure bred livestock breeders were hit by the depression of 1920. The bottom dropped out of the Poland China breeders' market. Long lines of people waited to draw their money out of banks before they closed. The bank in Goldfield foreclosed on its outstanding loans and many of the farmers lost their farms--as we did. We moved to nearby Goldfield for a year, then to Waterloo for two, and to Des Moines, where I finished my high school years while my parents struggled to make a living as best they could.

I can't remember that I learned much of anything for
the first ten years I was in school, but I must have because
I got promoted each year and I read a lot.   However, most
everyone passed each year, even the town's one retarded boy,
who was carried along until the ninth grade and then was allowed to drop out.

The only books in the Goldfield school, other than one's
textbooks, were a set of Dickens' novels and a dictionary--
though I never used the latter.   In fact there were very few
books in the whole town.   One family--the bank owners--gave
us boys access to their library.   The sets--the Tom Swifts,
Rover Boys and Zane Grey's books--were there.   But I doubt
if there were any books that "educated" us directly.   We did
borrow books from the Eagle Grove Public Library--five miles
away.   The trouble with that was that the road between Goldfield and Eagle Grove was a muddy morass part of the time
and we couldn't be sure of getting our library books back on
time, which meant overdue fines that we couldn't afford to
pay.   The result was that we didn't go there often.   Yet I
did read lots of books and magazines and my mother complained often that instead of doing my outside chores I would
"have my nose in a book. "   I do remember that I loved to
sprawl upside down in our big leather chair with a bowl of
popcorn and a book.   Later I learned to accept a horizontal,
and finally, a vertical position for reading.

The middle of my sophomore year (there were only
three of us in the class) my family moved to Waterloo, Iowa,
where I enrolled in the West Waterloo High School, a new,
very large urban school.   I was absolutely terrified, and I
think I spent most of that year in a state of shock.   I did
well on the parallel bars in gym, and I liked the indoor swimming pool (my first experience swimming in water that wasn't
muddy).   My junior year we moved to the east side of Waterloo, and I spent one year in the East Waterloo High School,
an older and less formidable school.   By then I was coming
out of my state of shock and my mind started to work.   I
found myself in a class called the Literature of the Bible,
taught by a beady-eyed old maid fundamentalist teacher, who
tried to teach us a literal interpretation of the Bible.   Just
where my skepticism came from, I never knew, but I began
to bait the teacher and argue with her.   She said she prayed
for me each night.

It was in Waterloo that I first learned about Judaism,
and I met my first Jewish friends--some of whom couldn't

play on Saturdays. The realization that there were other religions than Methodist Christianity hit me with a bang, and
woke me up.

My senior year in the North Des Moines High School
(where we had moved), a completely integrated high school
with high quality faculty and administration, was all new and
exciting, thanks in part to my home room teacher--a Mrs.
Rehret, an Oberlin graduate and a sister of Dr. Robert Mil-
likan, then one of the great physicists. I don't know what
she did to me, but whatever it was, it worked. I got As in
my classes (except in English, where the teacher tried to
make us read Milton), participated in senior class activities,
and even though I worked every afternoon and all day Saturdays selling shoes in a down town store, I seemed to have
had time for reading.

The high school librarian gave me Darwin's Origin of
the Species to read, and I became an instant atheist, convert-
ing as many of my classmates as possible. A librarian in
our branch library suggested that I read Robinson's The Modern Mind in the Making, which really set me free from the
torments of an adolescent boy. When I read that the mean-
derings of my mind were quite normal, I stopped worrying
about my sanity, or lack thereof.

OFF TO COLLEGE

My senior year in high school had opened enough doors to
the world of learning to get me pretty excited and I knew I
wanted to go to college, not to follow any specific profession
but simply to learn.   But where?   I knew I wanted to get
away from Iowa, although some of my fellow students were
going to go to Grinnell and Cornell, and a few to the University of Iowa.   My older brother, Clayton, had gone to Oberlin two years earlier and he was enthusiastic about it.   Mrs.
Rehret, my home room teacher, an Oberlin graduate, was
urging me to go there.   And then when her distinguished
brother, Robert A. Millikin, a Nobel Prize-winning physicist,
gave an assembly talk to us at North High, I knew that Oberlin was the place for me.

Soon after graduation, I left for Oberlin, arriving there
with $5.00 in my pocket.   I worked during the summer mow-
ing lawns and waiting tables at the Oberlin Inn.   I lived in a
boarding house with my brother and his friends, and sat in
on the discussions, which we called bull sessions.   I read
such books as André Maurois' Ariel and Sinclair Lewis's
Arrowsmith, all of which whetted my appetite to begin my
studies at Oberlin.

Although I suffered during my freshman year from the
mental growing pains of a college freshman when challenged
by a scholarly and stimulating faculty, my four years at Oberlin were just great, and the experience was the best thing that
could have happened to me at that time.   During the first two
years I stumbled often before I learned how to study in the
manner that produced good grades, as well as filling me full
of information, but during my last two years it all seemed to
come together.   At least six of my professors inspired me
to extra effort and pleasure.   One of them, Professor P. T.
Fenn, in a course in International Law, threw a group of
cases before us and told us to read them and then state the
legal principles found in them.   This was the first time I had
encountered inductive teaching, and I wondered why other faculty members didn't use it more.

But, even so, alas, I sometimes fell into temptations that hurt my grades. For example, one day I saw a set of Scott's Waverley Novels in a second-hand book store window and I bought it and spent much of my time the next two weeks reading those romantic tales--surely a foolish thing to do in terms of keeping up with my course work.

The college library book stacks were closed to undergraduates, but I got in anyway, and in my wanderings I ran into several shelves of Chinese poetry in English translation-- a realm I would never have discovered otherwise. I found the books fascinating and read many of them. Just how they happened to be there I never found out, except that Azariah Root, the librarian, was a great collector. Oberlin did have many ties with China, and perhaps that's the explanation.

The library had many of its books locked up in the departmental seminar rooms (a hangover from the German university library system, where many of Oberlin's science faculty members had done their graduate work), and these books were not available unless one were registered in the Seminar (Honors) courses, which I was not. I wanted very much to read G. Lowes Dickinson's The International Anarchy, which was in the Political Science Seminar. Had I gone in to the Librarian and made a strong plea for the book I'm sure I would have gotten it. But, like many undergraduates, I didn't know the Librarian, and I was afraid to ask.

These two experiences at Oberlin influenced my policies when I became a library director. Thus, the new library at the University of Colorado, opened for service early in 1940, was the first large university in the United States to operate on a fully open access basis (except for the rare books); and neither the University of Colorado nor the University of Iowa, where I was Director for fourteen years, allowed the faculty to lock up books in departmental seminars, as was done in most American universities, following the German pattern.

As I have said, when I arrived in Oberlin in June 1925, I had exactly $5.00 in my pocket, but I did have a waiter's job in the College Hotel dining room lined up. My second year I became head waiter, which gave me no more cash, but which taught me many things, including responsibility and the ability to watch a dining room full of people and to spot quickly a patron who wanted attention, even before he or she realized it. Unfortunately, the hotel dining room went broke the middle of my second year, and I had to seek other employment. I supplemented my board job by mowing lawns and by painting houses in the summer time, and during the school year by cleaning a faculty apartment three hours each day. The College allowed me to postpone paying much of my tuition until after I graduated (about $1,100.00 worth, I think). A local clothier allowed me to buy a pair of slacks and a few items on credit. I bought a class sweater, and wore this all during college. (My wife made me throw it away in Alamosa as soon as I had money enough to buy a jacket. And then, to her disgust, the apartment caretaker rescued the sweater from the trash can and wore it around the apartment for a few years.) I had one suit, purchased in high school years, and that was the last one until after I was graduated. A poor boy could go to a college like Oberlin without feeling discriminated against by his fellow students for lack of money.

My work schedule, plus the tremendously heavy reading requirements imposed by the faculty, left me physically tired most of the time. Oberlin's motto, "Learning and Labor," was not mere rhetoric. Football Saturdays were the worst, because not only did we have to serve a special lunch for the squad at the hotel, but the dining room on those nights was crowded until 8 p.m., after which we waiters took our dates to a college dance. I do remember that our girls were understanding about our fatigue.

It was customary for most students to study in the library afternoons and evenings. Some of us studied there with our dates each night. Theda and I studied in the Art Library, partly because there was more privacy than in the big reading room in the old Carnegie building. The girls had to be back in their dormitories by 9:40 (by 8 p.m. for freshwomen). Thus we usually left the library at 9:20, allowing ten minutes for walking and ten minutes for necking. Each couple had its own territory for such purposes and the rights were respected by others.

I had great difficulty deciding among English, History and Political Science for a major, and compromised by choosing pre-Journalism, which permitted me to combine all three subjects. I did give some thoughts to becoming a journalist and even talked with one of the editors of the Cleveland Press about it, but never did any more about it. I did take one course in Essay and Editorial Writing, taught by my favorite English professor, and found that I enjoyed writing essays.

Along came graduation time, and because I was in love

and had marriage in mind I began to think about how to make
a living, something that most Oberlin students never gave
much thought to while undergraduates. The pre-medics, of
course, were exceptions, but most of the rest of us were
concerned with what we thought of as a liberal education, or
possibly about going on to graduate school to learn a profession. I decided that I would like to be a high school English
teacher, but I had taken no courses in Education and consequently couldn't get a job. So I enrolled in the University of
Chicago Home Study Program for three courses in Education.
I did lesson plans after painting houses for ten hours during
the day. Mostly I could fill out the questions based on what
I had learned at Oberlin, but came September and I had not
finished any of the courses. So what to do? I decided to
go to Cleveland to find work.

My first day job-hunting I had two offers: one selling
shoes in Taylor's Department Store, and one as head of the
book store in the Burrows Brothers' University branch. I
chose the latter even though the pay was much less. I charged
into this job with great enthusiasm, thinking I could bring
book reading to the masses. The first thing I did (over the
protest of the head book buyer for the company) was to arrange a big window display of poetry books. Alas, it didn't
sell a single book of poetry. Then (since by fall the depression had hit) I arranged a display of business management
books with a stock market ticker tape running in the midst
of the display. Alas, again no buyers. After that I did no
more displays and confined my efforts to promoting books
that would sell. The clientele was strange. There were a
few wealthy women who would come in, swoop up an armful
of new books and dash out. Then there were young single
women, skinny, woebegone and obviously underfed, who looked
for titles that promised sex. Scarlet Sister Mary sold well
that year. The store manager had high standards and there
were some popular new titles we were not allowed to stock--
at least above the counter. One was The President's Daugh-
ter, all about President Harding's carryings on, and Chick
Sale's little book about outdoor privies, The Specialist, was
another.

Although books were cheap then, many of our customers had so little money that they couldn't buy them. I recall
one man who came in once a week to covet a $5.00 biogra-
phy of George Washington. He practically wore it out and
we finally sold it to him at cost--$3.00.

George F. Strong, Librarian of Adelbert College,
Western Reserve University, was a regular customer in the
evenings, and it was a pleasure to visit with him. (I worked
several nights a week.) When it came time for me to take
the final examinations for the three Chicago extension courses,
I asked him if he would serve as proctor for the exams. He
consented and we became better acquainted. He asked me
one evening if I had ever thought about becoming a librarian.
Of course I hadn't, but I became interested and decided to
go to the W. R. U. library school the next fall. I applied and
was admitted and started in September 1930. I had saved
enough money to pay my first semester's tuition and for the
second I was later awarded a Brett Memorial scholarship. I
had a board job at a nearby residential hotel for old crochety
people, and a student assistant's job at the University Library,
which paid for laundry and pocket money. I roomed with
Thomas Fleming, Walter Brahm and John Shenk. We sur-
vived--just barely.

LIBRARY SCHOOL

Since library schools of that period stressed the "how to" approach, the work was practical and no one thought about a philosophy of librarianship, or whether Library Science was a science or not. We were preparing ourselves to move into a job--if one existed.

That year as a class project in the Book Selection course, I read every book then available in the English language on the subject of politics and government in the Soviet Union and I wrote a heavily annotated bibliography on the subject. (Senator Joseph McCarthy never found out about that, by the way.) Since I was rather proud of the work, I showed it to Mr. Strong, who, after reading it, advised me, as I have said earlier, to keep on writing, a suggestion, some of my friends say, I have taken too literally. He also wanted a copy of my bibliography for the library, which of course pleased me.

Mr. Strong, besides being one of the kindest and most generous men I ever knew, was also very absent minded. One day when I was telling him about a report I had written, his phone rang. He picked up the phone and threw it into a desk drawer, and held my report up to his ear. He took Theda, my fiancée, and me to the Cleveland Club for lobster lunch, and as a wedding present, gave us six sterling silver demitasse spoons. And I was just a student assistant!

My interest in library building planning was probably born from an assignment given to me by Dean Herbert S. Hirshberg during the spring term of 1931. Western Reserve University was considering the purchase of a Jewish Settlement House adjacent to the campus. It was a huge, multi-storied building. My task was to find out how many books the building would hold. I was to work from the floor plans. I estimated the building's capacity by formula, and secondly by actually drawing in the bookstacks, on 4' 6" centers. The results from the two methods did not coincide and I learned my first lesson about the advantages and efficiencies

of open space.   The University purchased the building later,
but I never learned whether my calculations were of any use.
Probably not.

Relations between the student assistants and the regular library staff were close and personal, and I learned as
much from them as I did from my courses in the Library
School.   Night duty on the reserve desk involved more than
handing out books because there were no reference librarians
on duty at night and we had to take all kinds of questions.   I
recall how proud I was when in response to a question about
Russia, my knowledge of books about the USSR was put to use.
I didn't explain that this was an exception, not a fair measure of my competence in other areas.

When in August, I got my position at Adams State
College, and announced my intention to marry, the library
staff threw a week-end beach party on Lake Erie and presented us with a set of Coleport demitasse cups and a whole
bushel basket full of household gadgets, such as clothes pins,
screwdrivers, pliers, etc.   And then when we were married
August 25th in the Oberlin First Church, Mr. Strong closed
the University Library and the whole staff came to the wedding, including Mr. Strong.   And remember, I was just a
student assistant.   I mention this only as a measure of the
spirit of caring that existed at W. R. U. in 1931.

The Waples-Thompson Arguments

The C. S. Thompson attack on Douglas Waples and his reply
with follow-up comments by a variety of librarians in Library
Journal in 1931 attracted widespread attention in the profession, and was the first really exciting idea I had encountered
since going to Library School.

It is difficult in the year 1979 to explain what this ar-
gument between Waples and Thompson was all about because
we librarians have for years taken it for granted that all of
our activities are evaluated, explained and governed by whatever intellectual discipline or methodology is most relevant.
But this was not true in the years before 1931.   Most librarians tried to develop taste for fine writing by reading extensively in the Humanities and by knowing as many books as
possible.   Librarianship was the art of bringing together a
reader and the book he or she needed or wanted.   No one

thought very much about the efficiency of the mechanics of
the library's operations which were the background of the
scene of the joining of the reader and the book. Although
simple primers of a "how to" nature did exist, they were indeed simple and untouched by the methods of the basic disciplines. There seemed to be no need for the application of
the analyses we now must make. For example, one took for
granted the value of a university's having a large book collection. No one worried about the fact that possibly half of
the collection might not be used in a year's time. The cost
of space didn't seem important. Preoccupation with the mechanics of a library's operations would have been frowned
upon.

But then along came Waples and the other faculty of
the Graduate Library School saying that possibly the library
could do a better job if each aspect of its operation, including the reader, and even the non-reader, could be better understood. And that this understanding might come through the
application of the methods of scholarship of the various disciplines.

The older A. L. A. establishment members were strongly
pro-Thompson because they thought of librarianship as an art
which would be harmed by the kind of inquiries Dr. Waples
was interested in at the G. L. S. In reconsidering this issue,
which is by no means dead in 1979, one should remember
that up to 1931 the Humanities had pretty much dominated the
American universities. Deans and presidents came mostly
from the Humanities. It was in the 1920s that Professor
Paul Shorey, perhaps the most articulate and persuasive
spokesman for the Humanities, made the last major defenses
against the encroaching Social Sciences--which were rapidly
expanding their influence and research activities in the universities in the 1930s. Inquiries into the nature of human
endeavor, long the province of the Humanities, now attempted
to borrow the methods of the physical sciences with mixed
effectiveness. Grant money flowed freely to the Social Sciences
and distinguished Social Science departments were established,
especially in the newer Midwest state universities, and in the
University of Chicago.

Thus, it was not surprising that the G. L. S. at the
University of Chicago was established, not to train librarians
in the arts of librarianship, as the other library schools had
been doing, but to investigate those arts in relation to the individuals and institutions they were created to serve, and to

the records of civilization they attempted to collect, organize, preserve and make available for use.

C. S. Thompson, Librarian of the University of Pennsylvania, speaking for the many middle-aged and older librarians (most of whom had been educated in the Humanities) protested that a "science" of librarianship would destroy the practice of librarianship, which he considered to be a personal relationship between the librarians full of knowledge of books and readers, on a one-to-one basis. His attack centered on Douglas Waples, whose specialties might have been called the Sociology of Reading. Thompson misunderstood what Waples was trying to do, which really had nothing to do with the training of librarians or with what a practicing librarian would do qua librarian. The G. L. S. and its program were intelligently defended by such distinguished librarians as John Christian Bay and C. S. Williamson.

The debates sort of petered out but the issues continued to smolder mildly. The publication of Pierce Butler's Introduction to Library Science in 1933 did much to spread a sensible interpretation of what a science of librarianship could mean to the profession and the issue moved into the background, although now and then when the moon is full someone feels inclined to have another go at defining his philosophy of librarianship.

MY EXPERIENCES AT THE GRADUATE LIBRARY SCHOOL, UNIVERSITY OF CHICAGO, 1934-1937

In terms of my own development, the intellectual discipline at the University of Chicago was exactly what I needed at the time. A liberal education at Oberlin and professional training at W. R. U. were essential, but alone not enough to equip one for a university-level library career. The School saw to it that we learned, from courses both within and outside the School, the methods of research in the Sciences, the Social Sciences and the Humanities. We all had to learn statistical methods and we could choose to study these courses in the Business School, the Department of Psychology, the School of Education or the Department of Economics, all of which had nationally known professors teaching the courses. I tried W. F. Osburn in the Department of Economics, but I couldn't hack it--I simply couldn't do the mathematics. But to make up for my failure I sat in on lectures in the other deartments. During one of the reading periods I studied the textbooks on statistics, and from these I learned that advanced statistics were not for me. And I never have tried to use anything except the most elementary measures of central tendencies. I did learn enough about statistics to know that some of the current writers in our library journals, who use elaborate formulas and mathematical models, are using cannons to shoot mice. Calculations are sometimes carried out to the second figure beyond the decimal point, when the data probably don't justify accuracy beyond the first whole number.

The courses I took within the G. L. S. with Waples, Butler, Randall and Wilson were substantial, challenging, enlightening, and taught at the graduate level. But it wasn't the course work at Chicago that was important. It was the spirit of inquiry and the research going on everywhere in the University. Students, even undergraduates, were drawn into the research projects with such men as Lloyd Warner and his Yankee City studies, or Louis Wirth and his racial studies in South Chicago. It seemed to me that every faculty member I knew was deeply involved in some exciting inquiry and they brought their students into their work.

Another thing, it was a tradition at Chicago for faculty members to be in their offices or studies or laboratories all day with open doors. None of this business of notices posted on doors, "office hours Thursdays 11-12." One could drop in and talk with them. And of course one could savor greatness just by walking down the corridors and reading name-plates like Park, Burgess, Knight, Holzinger, Ogburn, Thurstone, Thornton Wilder, Paul Douglas. And the public lectures Paul Douglas and Thornton Wilder gave were exceedingly popular. One couldn't help being drawn into the heady atmosphere at Chicago.

In retrospect, as I said, the courses we took within the G. L. S. seem not to have been nearly as important as the various research projects being carried out by the faculty. Perhaps this explains the difference in students' judgment of the faculty. For example, my only contact with Carleton Joeckel was in the classroom (because his research was in the public library field) and here it seemed to me he was outside the spirit of G. L. S. Perhaps I would have felt differently if I had done research with him--but I doubt it.

Although I did no research with Leon Carnovsky, it was clear that he was in the groove of G. L. S. 's spirit of inquiry. One incident that happened to me in one of his classes made me self-conscious with him ever after. I wrote a book review of a certain book for him as a class project. Weeks after, I happened to read in one of the older issues of Library Journal a review of the same book and it was very similar to the one I had written. To my horror I realized that I must have read the printed review earlier and subconsciously repeated it in my review. At least while writing my review I had no remembrance of having read the earlier one. I rushed to Carnovsky and explained the situation. He said he had noticed the similarity and accepted my explanation, but I never knew whether or not he really believed me. His shyness with people made it difficult for me to get to know him very well. On the last day of the 1936 A. L. A. Conference in Denver my wife and I took Dr. Carnovsky for a drive up to Estes Park and over the newly opened Trail Ridge Road. I didn't judge the time too well and we found ourselves in a race with time down the then unpaved South Saint Vrains Canyon to get Leon to his train. He rushed to his room to pack and gave me his wallet to pay his hotel bill. I guess he trusted me or he wouldn't have done that. We got him to the depot with no time to spare. He and Douglas Waples understood each other well, and together represented the kind of research Mr. Thompson had called "scientific."

Pierce Butler's Introduction to Library Science course was taken by all new students. His lectures were substantial, mature and challenging to most of us, except when now and then he injected a little of his conservative political philosophy--which I think he did to see if we were awake. His point of view, embodied in his Introduction to Library Science book, was that the range of activities and materials in a library was sufficiently wide to provide subjects for research using the methodologies of all the major disciplines in the world of scholarship, and that it would be good for the profession if these activities and materials were subjected to appropriate research by those who were qualified and interested. He also made clear that this point of view of library education was not in conflict with the kind of training one got in the other library schools. The latter was necessary for all, but the G. L. S. was important for those who were interested in the whys of library behavior.

My contacts with Mr. Butler were minimal outside the one course I took with him. Thus, when after I had completed the writing for my Preliminaries Mr. Butler congratulated me, I was considerably surprised and pleased.

Professor William Randall never bored us in class by making us listen to rehashes of the professional literature, nor did he make us read all that stuff. Instead he put us to work on small research projects in academic librarianship. His influence on me was strong and useful. And there was a personal reason for this--in the fall of 1936 a member of the Faculty Library Committee at the University of Colorado denounced, at a meeting of the Faculty Senate, the way in which Mr. Smith was running the library and demanded an investigation. As a result President Norlin asked Mr. Randall to come out and make a survey. One of Randall's recommendations was that an Associate Director be appointed to take charge and he recommended me for the position. Mr. Smith, apparently remembering the good turn I had done for him earlier, agreed and so I was appointed, to take office the next June after I had finished my doctorate.

Professor Douglas Waples was clearly the most innovative member of the faculty in terms of the "scientific" spirit. Even though I probably should have chosen a dissertation subject in the field of academic librarianship with Dr. Randall, I found myself working with Waples. His course in research methods was useful but it was in working on his research projects that we got the most from him. The South Chicago and

St. Louis studies data were thrown at us and we were challenged to select a dissertation problem from them. Most students were afraid of Waples because they didn't know how to cope with him in conference. His method was to start talking on a subject and then let one idea lead to another until sometimes neither he nor his listeners knew where he was. He had in mind that bright people would challenge him when he got off base too far. Most of the students didn't seem to realize that, and would say nothing. He also had a habit of speaking without blinking his eyes and he talked in a monotone. He sort of hypnotized some people. He probably wrote those people off as not worth wasting his time with. At any rate he and I got along fine, but I'll have to admit that my wife's work with Waples was better than mine.

Waples discovered that my wife played the cello, so we were invited to participate in the Waples Saturday night musicals, at which he and his daughters and wife all played musical instruments, he with his oboe, Theda with the cello and his daughters with violin and clarinets. He employed Theda to work with him on the New York Regents study and on other projects, and he soon found that talking out his ideas with her was invaluable because he couldn't stampede her and she made him talk sense, which was just the kind of help he wanted. Waples was, indeed, a great man.

Although completely different in personality and background, Dean Louis Round Wilson had great influence on those of us who worked with him. His course laid on heavy reading assignments but, like Randall, he didn't bore us with rehashing the same material in class. Instead, he illustrated the problems from his own widely varied experience and by the reports each of us was required to make. His sense of humor permeated everything he did. For example, one day in class a young man from the South came to class unprepared to make the report he was supposed to make. He tried to bluff it through. Wilson sat there smiling and chuckling while the student went further and further out on a limb, with his face becoming redder and redder, until finally he had to stop. Wilson just laughed and so did we, and I doubt if that person ever tried to bluff again.

It was Wilson's wisdom and humor that carried the School through that difficult period, because there had been dissension among the faculty on the very issue C. Thompson had raised, and on the question of the School's curriculum. What Dean Wilson did was to arrange it so that each faculty

member could do his work without being attacked by others,
and so that the students didn't get penalized by choosing to
work under any one of the faculty.

My wife worked for Dean Wilson, too, on one of his
research projects, and he, too, found her intelligence and
human understanding useful.   One time as they sat in his office he admitted that he couldn't understand what Waples was
talking about on some point, and did she?   She did, and her
explanation satisfied him.

Recently it has been claimed that Dean Wilson sub-
verted the original "scientific" intent of the G. L. S.   It was
true that he introduced measures that would increase the enrollment, the School's income, and a larger class from which
to recruit graduate students for the Ph. D.-level work, which
continued, undiminished, in the original spirit.   During my
three years there the Dean did many things to lessen the an-
tagonism of the A. L. A. old guard toward the School, including serving as President of A. L. A.

During my first semester, in addition to the introductory courses we were all expected to take, I managed to pass
both my German and French language exams, thanks to the
excellent courses I had taken at Oberlin.   Thus, in contrast
to the experience of many of the other students in my class
who had difficulties with the language examinations, I was
free sooner to begin preparing myself for the Preliminary
examinations that ordinarily were taken the spring of one's
second year.   One had to pass these before being admitted
to the Dissertation program.   One prepared for them by extensive reading in addition to the course work.

After my first year at Chicago I was assigned to Dean
Wilson's Geography of Reading project as part of my fellowship.   I worked closely with G. Flint Purdy on the project.
Wilson's directions were always clear and not difficult to follow.   The purpose of the study was to analyze and describe
on a regional basis the availability of reading resources and
other social and economic resources that might be related to
the distribution of reading.   We worked all day in Room #10,
a large room filled with Monroe calculating machines and
National Youth Administration students working for Waples under my wife's direction.   The noisy clattering of the machines
plus the inevitable conversations of the students meant that in
order to survive one had to develop strong powers of concentration.   I survived but the penalty I paid in later life was

being accused of being absent minded--which, of course, is
nothing more than the back of the mirror called concentration.

My three years at Chicago were a good mixture of
hard work, intellectual growth and satisfaction, and a happy
family life. Our first year, after paying our tuition, we had
$77. 77 left to live on for each month. Sometimes we would
have enough money left at the end of the month to ride the
"L" to the Loop and window shop, but never enough to buy
anything. Occasionally we and the Purdys would go to a bar
on Cottage Grove Avenue and order mugs of beer, which along
with the corned beef sandwiches they served free with the
beer, substituted for one meal those days--beer 15¢, sandwich
free, one meal for two, 30¢ plus 10¢ tip.

I refreshed my bank account slightly by returning for
the summer of 1935 to my position at Adams State College,
and for the summer of 1936 by serving as Library Advisor
to graduate students at the Colorado State Teachers College
in Greeley, which had just announced a new program for the
Master's degree, substituting three field reports for the usual
thesis requirement. The trouble was that they provided no
preparatory training for the students. It was my job to help
them learn how to do a field report--some 75 of them. This
did not seem too difficult for me and I had rather good success with the students--or so many of them told me. Prior
to my summer in Greeley I had resigned my position at Adams State on the assumption that when my doctoral work was
finished I would find a larger position.

Finances were somewhat less tight my second and third
years because the fellowship paid more and because my wife's
earning could be used to finance trips to the opera, the sym-
phony concerts, the ballets, and even for a splurge in a restaurant now and then.

On Sundays we would get our car out of the garage and
drive it along the Outer Drive enough to keep the battery
charged up. And there were occasional parties with our
friends. Of course, there was much free entertainment at
the University and we never felt deprived. For example, one
year Elizabeth S. Coolidge sponsored the Pro Arte String
Quartet, playing the entire cycle of Beethoven string quartets.
We went to the whole series. Also, every day there were
lectures at the University, all of which were free. So, entertainment was rich, abundant and inexpensive.

One of our friends, a student in biochemistry, would occasionally be able to buy pure grain alcohol at a very low price, and this we could mix with orange juice for a Saturday night party. One fall, Flint Purdy and I made a few gallons of grape wine from grapes Flint got in Michigan. We did the fermenting in our kitchen. Unfortunately we moved to another apartment because across the light well separating us from other apartments lived a young couple who fought every night until nearly 2 a. m. Most of the swear words they flung at each other were new to my wife--a city girl, you may recall--and I had to explain them to her (I had learned them from the hired men on our farm). Finally the lack of sleep was too much for us and we moved out. But carrying the wine jugs across the Midway increased the fermentation and the corks would blow with a loud bang just as we met other people, thus causing a degree of hilarity that nearly did us in by the time we reached the other apartment. The wine turned out to be too sweet.

The faculty decided I was ready to take my Preliminaries the spring of my second year, although I never knew just how they decided this. I got so hyped up for these examinations, which consisted of sixteen hours of writing, that I actually enjoyed the writing and when I got through I felt that I had done well. To illustrate how hyped up I was I recall resenting the fact that Dr. Waples attended a Beethoven String Quartet concert when, in my fevered opinion, he should have stayed home reading my examination papers! Fortunately I kept my opinion to myself. After a week or so I was told that I had passed. The reaction then set in and I was so weary I yawned constantly for a month. The orals, after the dissertation was completed, were by contrast not difficult.

At that period in G. L. S. history each person elected his course program (with faculty approval, of course) around the area of his dissertation interest. Thus my courses were with George Works in Higher Education, Lloyd Warner in Anthropology, Louis Wirth in Sociology, and I even sat in on a course in Vector Analysis taught by Louis Thurstone. Also, I took at least one course with each faculty member in the Graduate Library School.

I decided to do my dissertation with Waples on the general subject of the distribution of print, using the data from the South Chicago and St. Louis studies. I was to try to find out what kind of publications each typical distributing agency distributed to people grouped into categories by age, sex, kind of employment, educational background, etc.

Writing a dissertation with Waples was a nightmare, but a fascinating one for me. Each idea in our discussions led to several more ideas, each of which had to be considered, and each of which led to more ideas. Soon, the biggest problem was to keep the scope of the project under control--unless one were willing to spend the rest of his life writing a dissertation. This was wonderful training because that is the biggest problem everyone faces in his professional life. Ars longa, vita brevis.

At one point my mind went completely blank from fatigue. I could do nothing. I went home and we probably went to a movie, or something, for a couple of days, and then I was okay again. I stiffened my jaw and resisted Waples' best efforts to sidetrack me. By late February of my third year I had the dissertation written, approved, and ready for typing. I looked forward to a peaceful spring in Chicago.

However, in March, Mr. C. H. Smith, the Librarian at the University of Colorado, died unexpectedly and I was asked if I could take over, even though I wasn't due to go there until June. I made arrangements for my wife to remain in Chicago to finish her work with Wilson and Waples, and to see that my dissertation got passed along to the faculty for their final comments. Professor Joeckel objected to this arrangement, but the rest of the faculty approved, so I left for Boulder.

One night a fire broke out in the apartment building adjacent to the one my wife was living in, and she was forced to evacuate her apartment in the middle of the night, carrying Waples' cello under one arm, and her portable sewing machine under the other. She spent several hours sitting on the curb protecting her possessions until it was safe to re-enter the apartment. What wives won't do for their husbands!

Later in the spring I returned for my final orals, which turned out to be pretty pro forma and a distinct anticlimax. My defense of the dissertation seemed pretty silly to me, as I am sure it did to the faculty. But they said I had passed, probably because they didn't know what else to do with me. It seemed at the time, and still does, that the G. L. S. experience was a wonderful one, and it proved to be a major turning point in my life.

SEVEN YEARS AT THE UNIVERSITY OF COLORADO, 1937-44

My predecessor at the University of Colorado had been given so many non-library responsibilities (raising money for a student union building, managing a geology science lodge in the mountains, serving as faculty representative to the athletic conference, and refereeing at college football games) that he had little time for the library, which needed reorganizing from top to bottom. I plunged in with great self-confidence and enthusiasm. I had Dr. Randall's report to start with, and the other changes that needed to be made seemed obvious and easy. I soon located a fine Associate Director (Henry Waltemade at the University of Illinois); a Head Cataloger (Victoria Siegfried Barker, a Stanford and Berkeley graduate, at Idaho State); and Ray Swank (a student at Western Reserve Library School). Leroy Merritt joined us the next summer. These bright, young and enthusiastic librarians soon got the technical operations of the library on a sound basis.

In 1938 we had a large WPA project going in the library, with as many as one hundred workers at one time. In abilities and qualifications they ranged from holders of Ph. D. s to unskilled workers. I put Ray Swank in charge of this project, and this turned out to be a wise decision, because with his genial patience and genuine interest in people, Ray soon won the love and respect of the crew--who did everything from rubbing lanolin and neat's foot oil (mixed in our home kitchen in spite of the smell) into the sheepskin bindings of the Congressional set and other leather bindings (including some artificial leathers that wouldn't absorb it), to rather complicated cataloging and serials recording. All government documents had been classified and cataloged into the regular book collection. Ray, with his crew, pulled them out and reclassified the federal documents into the U. S. Superintendent of Documents classification. Since there was no parallel classification system for state documents, Ray developed one --which was widely circulated and used; according to Ray, he still gets requests for copies of his classification.

Ray was much beloved by his WPA crew. He listened
to their personal problems, which were many, and he encour-
aged each person. When Ray announced he was resigning to
attend the Graduate Library School, the WPA crew threw a
party for him. Each person brought a present, even if nothing more than a tearful goodbye with a kiss on the cheek.

Ray later told me that he was the last of his Western
Reserve University class to be placed. We paid him, as I
recall, $1,300.00 per year. He would have been a bargain
at $10,000.00 a year.

Ray was a musician and a "night" person. He played
the organ in one of the churches and was also an excellent
pianist. But eight a.m. was not his best hour. By nine he
was awake and by ten he was going strong. He did remarkably good work, and a lot of it, too. I take great pride in
having recognized his talents and for giving him his first position. He is, in my judgment, one of the fine librarians
of the post-war period.

Soon after my arrival at Colorado, President Norlin
informed me that we were to have a new library building and
that I should get busy with the planning. After surveying the
literature I made a trip east to talk with Joseph B. Wheeler,
a well-known expert on library buildings, and with Mr. C.
A. Klauder, a Philadelphia architect who had a life contract
with the University of Colorado. Wheeler gave me sound advice and taught me how to go about the planning process.
Since I had expressed an interest in the subject divisional
plan, I studied the Enoch Pratt Library in Baltimore and
found it good. Wheeler advised me to consult with Alfred
Githens, who, together with Angus Macdonald, had written the
1932 basic idea for "unit" (now called modular) libraries.

Mr. Klauder, though friendly and genial, had many
strange ideas about university libraries, including the idea
that it was wrong to give students easy access to books--his
theory being that students wouldn't appreciate anything that
was easy to obtain. He promised to begin planning the C.U.
library.

On my own responsibility, I invited Angus Macdonald
to come to Boulder to discuss the unit system concept--which
had been used to a limited extent in the Library of Congress
Annex and was being considered, in modified form, at the
Colorado State College of Education--which did use the idea

in its 1938 addition.　Macdonald convinced me that if the concept were improved, it could be used for an entire university library building.

　　Although I pushed the modular idea hard at Boulder (going so far as to make a layout of an entire building, which unfortunately got lost when I moved to Iowa), Mr. Klauder refused even to consider it.　He informed the Board of Regents that the concept stifled the architect's fancy and that if they wanted to use it, he would resign.　That put an end to modular planning for Colorado.

　　In fact, I had very little influence on the design of the Colorado library, except that at my request, Mr. Klauder did thicken the building somewhat.　He did, to his credit, work out a reasonable version of a building that would house my conception of a subject divisional arrangement, but, of course, in a fixed function building with a multi-tier bookstack separating two wings of equal size.

　　The divisional plan was to be a substitute for the traditional university library organization based on type of function--reference, reserve, circulation, etc.　I got the idea from existing examples:　the Cleveland Public Library, the Enoch Pratt Library, Raney's ideas for a library at Johns Hopkins University, the University of Chicago Social Science Library and the University of California Biological Sciences Library.

　　At the Graduate Library School I had come to see that if the services of a librarian were to be truly helpful to advanced students and scholars, they would have to be given by librarians who had a deeper understanding of the subjects involved than was possessed by the typical librarian with an A. B. and B. S. in L. S.　But the majority of universities could not afford to provide expert librarians for each subject department.　The divisional plan was to be a compromise between the too-wide span of general reference librarians and the too-narrow span in departmental libraries.　And it was to give reference librarians responsibility over all types of publications within a subject division.　There were to be the usual three divisional libraries:　humanities, social sciences and sciences, each of which was to include a core collection of some 20,000 of the most used books in the division, including reference books, journals, reserves, etc.　And below the divisional libraries there was to be a lower divisional library, based on the University of Chicago Library in Cobb

Hall, whose services and collections were to be geared to the needs of freshman-level students. The subject divisional libraries were to be for majors and graduate students, with the research collections to be kept in the stacks, connected to each divisional reading room. The technical processing work for the materials in each division was to be done within the division, so that the processing librarians would have closer contact with readers of the division, and thus understand their needs better.

The Colorado plan differed from the Brown University divisional plan (neither university knew that the other had such ideas until a year after both were in operation) in that each division in Colorado included a fairly large core of books, whereas at Brown there were only reference books in each division.

The Colorado plan attracted much attention, partly because the building was indeed handsome, and partly because the plan offered something new. I became an instant expert on library building planning!

We moved into the Library during the Christmas vacation holiday of 1939, with the help of a loyal and hardworking crew of student assistants. Since the multi-tier book stacks in the old building were to be torn down and reassembled in the new building, there was a problem of where to put the books during the transition. A student came up with the solution: to use the planks from the football stadium seats, mounted on cement blocks. That's what we did for several weeks while the stacks were being moved.

Our first child, a boy, was born the second week in January 1940. The excitement caused by his arrival (we had waited several years for him), plus the pretty well sublimated fear that the subject divisional reading room plan might not work, got to me and I developed stomach ulcers. (When our second son, David, was born in 1944, I didn't get quite so excited.)

The ulcer first hit me one morning after a breakfast of undercooked trout, wheat cakes and fried eggs on a trout fishing trip with Malcolm Wyer, Carl Milan and Angus Macdonald. That morning we were scheduled to make a four-mile horseback ride to Hour Glass Lake above Fort Collins. I held things up for an hour while I sat in the outdoor privy battling the ulcer pains, not knowing quite what was wrong

with me. Since the other three men had eaten the same
breakfast, with no discernible effects, I was determined that
if they could do it, I could. I couldn't! Anyway, we all,
except Angus Macdonald, caught our limit of trout on dry flies.
I think Angus's poor vision kept him from knowing when to
set the hook, and caused him thus to miss all his strikes--
the only time I ever saw Angus completely frustrated.

When I got home I discussed my ulcer problem with
President Norlin. He suggested that I spend a month or so
with him resting at the Faculty Ranch--a kind of fishing camp
and mountain cabin retreat not far from Boulder. Access to
the Ranch was over a steep, rocky, one-way road, just barely
navigable by an ordinary car (the pre-jeep days). No tele-
phones. No electricity. Each of the cabins had its own well.
I stayed in Dr. Norlin's guest cabin. Weekends my wife
drove up from Boulder with a week's supply of groceries, and
she stayed the weekends with us.

Except for an occasional game of poker, and daily fishing, we did little but talk, eat and read. Some days we daw-
dled over our morning coffee until it was time for lunch.
Cooking and washing dishes constituted our chores. Once a
week we swept the floors. (It cured the ulcer.)

Dr. Norlin, a distinguished scholar in Greek literature,
was retiring after a long presidency during which he won the
love and respect of the entire University community. It was
his custom to spend much of his summer at the Faculty
Ranch, resting, reading and writing. He was, during this
period, doing everything he could to warn Coloradoans of the
coming danger of Hitler and Naziism, and of the need to come
to the aid of England. America at that time was feeling very
isolationist. Norlin learned of the Nazi danger during the
years 1932-33 while he held the Roosevelt professorship at
the University of Berlin. He saw at first hand the coming
tragedy of Hitlerism. As he said in the Preface in Things
in the Saddle (Harvard University Press, 1940):

> ...I witnessed the advance and triumph of Hitlerism.
> I was in a position, having ready access to many
> reliable sources of information, to penetrate beneath
> the glamorous surface of the sinister flood which
> swept away the old Germany and made room for the
> third Reich, with its sublimation of the savage in
> man and its deliberate mobilization on a national
> scale of that savagery against all the moral restraints

and decencies which civilization in the true sense
of the word has built up to make human life toler-
able on this not-too-kindly planet. It was a rather
terrible experience to be in the midst of a centuries-
old civilization going so swiftly to ruin, crash upon
crash; for one could not brush away the question
that came back again and again like a persistent
fly: if this could happen in Germany, could it not
happen elsewhere?

Early in his presidency in the 1920s the KKK controlled
the Colorado Legislature and many state offices. The KKK
threatened to cut off an appropriation to the University unless
Dr. Norlin would fire the Jews and Catholics on the faculty.
He refused, saying that the University would prefer to get
along without the money. The KKK beat a hasty retreat.

Those weeks with Dr. Norlin had a profound, but impossible to define, influence on my thinking. And I learned
how to go out on limbs without getting ulcers! For example,
I have tried to follow Dr. Norlin's advice about vacations.
When he was being interviewed for the presidency of the University he was asked if he thought he could do the job if he
worked eleven months a year. He replied that he couldn't,
but if he worked nine months a year he was sure he could.

We did fish for trout each day. One evening while
fishing at dusk my fly unexpectedly caught on a spruce tree
branch--not an unusual occurrence for a clumsy angler like
me. I climbed up to release the fly only to find my hand
grasping a bat, which had grabbed my fly in mid-air and then
flown into the tree to eat it. I screamed, fell out of the tree
and stepped on my fly rod. Dr. Norlin suggested that I
should be flattered by the fact that my fly, which I had tied,
had deceived the bat.

Following my summer at the Faculty Ranch with President Norlin I found myself deeply involved with making the
adjustments that are inevitable in a new university library
building, especially one that contained innovations. Although
the University community--especially the students--liked studying in the new Library, there were problems that soon became evident. First, the distinctions between the humanities
and the historical social sciences books were hard to draw
exactly, and there were too many places where a reader might
logically expect to find a given book, without looking in the
card catalog for its location. Since we couldn't afford to place

location symbols on all the cards for books not in the stacks, but only for the main entry, and since the term main entry meant different things to different people, the system chased people around too much if they happened to miss the location symbols in the catalog.

Secondly, since the building was a fixed-function one, the size of the various reading rooms didn't necessarily match the needs of the three divisions, nor could they be changed in size or arrangement.

Thirdly, we couldn't afford to buy the number of duplicates needed to bridge the gap among the divisions, or the reference books that had to be duplicated. It became tiresome to debate with faculty member about where "their" books should be located.

Nevertheless, the C. U. building worked well and was much liked by the students and faculty who used it. Many liked the divisional plan. Visitors seemed enthusiastic.

Three years experience with the plan, before I left for Iowa late in 1943, taught me that the best part of the subject divisional plan was the kind of reference service it permitted, not the separation of the book collection into specific subject groups. Even in libraries where books are shelved in a straightforward classification arrangement, classification systems are difficult to use. Interruptions in the classification system merely complicate an already complicated situation. In short, a central staff of subject divisional experts, each responsible for a given divisional area, with the book collections arranged in classification order in a modular building would be the right way to plan a university library. The question of whether the reference experts were to be placed in a central pool, or decentralized, as they were later at the University of Chicago and Indiana University, seemed open to further study.

ANOTHER CHANCE AT MODULAR PLANNING AT IOWA

I made the decision to leave the University of Colorado for the University of Iowa in 1943 for many reasons, some of which in retrospect were mere rationalizations, and some normal for an ambitious librarian thirty-two years of age. The University of Colorado was not a member of the Association of American Universities, whereas Iowa was. I thought I could have more influence in the profession on some of the issues that interested me, such as centralized cataloging, if I were in an A. A. U. university that was also a member of the Association of Research Libraries. Also, I wanted to be involved with a large library and I was not perceptive enough to anticipate the growth that would take place in Colorado following World War II. Salary levels had some influence. Also, I was convinced that Colorado was dominated by more "kooks" per square mile than any other part of the country except California. I was right about that and it's still true today. But whereas Colorado's kookiness led to many liberal and interesting experiments in government in the 1930s, today it results only in stupid, uninformed Republican conservatism.

At any rate, I did decide to take the Directorship of the University of Iowa Libraries in 1943.

Although I had had to lick my wounds at Klauder's rejection of modular planning for the Colorado building, I had not lost faith in the concept. Thus, when Iowa persuaded me that I ought to come there and do a modular building for them, I again asked Angus Macdonald to pay me a visit in Boulder before I left for Iowa, to talk about the possibilities for the proposed building at Iowa and to bring the technique up to date. This he did with the advice of Gilbert Fish, a New York structural engineer. The concept of the module, by the spring of 1944, was expanded to its most economical dimension when used with dry construction (as opposed to reinforced concrete. This turned out to be $19\frac{1}{2}$ by 27 feet.

The politically appointed architects for the Iowa library

objected to Macdonald's construction method of hollow columns, but they worked out an adaptation which used separate air ducts alongside the supporting columns. Horizontal distribution of the air was to be carried within the horizontal girders and brought down through a perforated suspended ceiling. Something went wrong in estimating the size of the air ducts and the result was that the supply of air in the Iowa building was inadequate.

Some architects objected to the low ceilings--eight feet. In fact one of them expressed his scorn by referring to the humpback ideas that came out of studying under the low ceilings in the Iowa library. Nobody at Iowa seemed to be conscious of the low ceilings.

An extremely low budget for the first unit of the Iowa library ($700,000) led to Spartan treatment both outside and inside. Metal pre-fabricated walls had to be used on one-half of the exterior. Inside, the finished ceiling had to be omitted on the second and third levels. The result was that the electrical wiring hung down below the girders. The building did not make a very impressive appearance. Nevertheless, it functioned as well as we had hoped.

The lessons I had learned at Colorado I applied at Iowa. There was a central core of reference librarians, each with a background of graduate work in a subject field somewhat broader than one department; the book collection was arranged in straight classification order, except for the rare books, the reserves and the Heritage Library.

The last was a brainstorm of mine. I thought it would be interesting and possibly instructive, if the books in a lower divisional library could be arranged in recognizable historical periods, on the assumption that by working in the midst of books in all subjects in one period of time, a student would absorb a feeling for the intellectual events of each time. I had in mind setting up physical exhibits of the arts and culture as well as the technology of each period, so that a multi-visual impact would be added to that of the contents of the books. We grouped the books by the following periods: "Early Man," "Greek and Roman," "Middle Ages," "Renaissance and Reformation," "17th," "18th," "19th" centuries and "Modern."

The idea made sense for the periods up through the Renaissance and Reformation periods, but after that the distinctions among the periods blurred. Had we been able to develop the visual exhibits, the plan would have been more impressive. Whether or not the concept helped the students I do not know, but personally I found it helpful to look at the books of great authors together with those of their contemporaries in other subjects. However, not everybody cares about those time relationships. Some of the Social Science faculties objected to the whole concept of the historical approach--a sort of Henry Ford "History is bunk" point of view. After a couple of years we abandoned the concept and arranged the books in straight classification order.

Although I was unable either at Colorado or Iowa to carry out the idea of fusing the technical processing and reference staffs, we did get some of the potential benefit of such fusing by having the processing people who were qualified spend part of their time at the reference desk. It is interesting to note that current developments in centralized cataloging through the Library of Congress MARC project and such networking as the Ohio College Library Center are making the fusing of the two staffs inevitable, regardless of theories for or against.

Since Iowa was the first large all-modular building, interest in the plan was widespread even before the building was constructed. To save time in explaining what it was all about I got Donald Bean to join in writing a small booklet which we mimeographed under the title, Modular Planning for College and Small University Libraries in 1945. As I recall, I did the text and Donald did the floor layouts. We distributed a lot of these booklets, probably because this was the first of its kind on modular planning. At $1.50 per copy we made enough money to buy an occasional bottle of whiskey to go with the poker games we held at ARL meetings. The booklet was reprinted several times before we let it be sold through the University Microfilms, Inc. out-of-print service.

How come this booklet was written five years before the Iowa library building was constructed? Well, the Iowa legislature sat around all that time waiting for a post-war depression to set in, until finally they realized their Republican ideas about economics were obsolete. They finally financed the first unit.

One amusing incident occured in this publication's history: Dr. Wladyslaw Piasecki, Librarian of the Krakow School

of Mines (now Krakow University), in 1958 translated the
booklet into Polish and published it without our authorization.
He then sent me a copy with a page inserted with Don's and
my pictures and signed it, "I dedicate you this copy hoping
you are merciful, to the Pirate, Wladyslaw Piasecki. " We
were indeed merciful and delighted, as we were when he visited us later.   His library, by the way, was the first in Europe to use modular planning.

Since 1951, when the Iowa building was finished, the
modular method has been almost universally used in this
country, and increasingly so in Great Britain and Europe.
Occasionally, the librarians who have failed to learn their
planning history pine for the good old days of grand stairways
and elegant reading rooms with high ceiling.   And then there
are architects who, like Charles Klauder, feel that "the concept restricts their fancy. " Perhaps there is some esoteric
connection between this turning back and the current (1979)
mood of ultra conservatism that appears to be sweeping the
country.

PROJECTS I WAS INVOLVED WITH AT IOWA, 1944-1958

The Midwest Inter-library Center
(now Center for Research Libraries)

When this project was first proposed by the President of Purdue University, its justification was largely as a central storage facility for little-used books in the Big Ten Universities. The first board set up to implement the idea was an equal mixture of university top administrators and university librarians. A committee of six was appointed to develop specific programs. A subcommittee of three, Colwell of Chicago, McDiarmid of Minnesota and I from Iowa, did the preliminary drafting. McDiarmid, Norman Kilpatrick and I were another subcommittee that worked on some ideas for centralized processing for the Center.

There were several points of view among the head librarians of the Big Ten Universities about the purpose and value of the Center. Two of them looked on it as a possible threat to their intent to make their libraries very large. Remember this was a time when universities were proud of the size and strength of their libraries and still spoke of them as being the heart of the universities, not as they do today, as a stone around their necks, or as bottomless pits! Several of the librarians were indifferent. Several looked on the Center as a place to dump their junk. I placed little value on the Center as a storage place for little used books, and high value on the possibilities of central acquisition projects as a means of increasing the bibliographical strength of the region; that is, that the Center would purchase, and keep in the Center for all to use, special collections no one library could afford. This was not a popular idea among my colleagues. Perhaps this was easy for me because I didn't feel any deep emotional ties to the University of Iowa, whereas some of my colleagues did have such ties with their universities. E. W. McDiarmid of Minnesota shared my opinions on this matter and several others said they would go along. But when a test came: the possibility of purchasing a large music history collection, the members said "No." One of the member libraries purchased the collection. I also took the position that the Center should, as soon as possible, become national in scope. My position was restated in the dedication remarks:

> It would be a rash librarian indeed who thought that his solutions to the specific tasks facing the Midwest Inter-Library Center would appear reasonable the day after tomorrow, or even tomorrow. The amount of thinking, talking, committee-sitting, and plain old-fashioned bickering among fallible university presidents and librarians that has been necessary to bring us this far--and a truly small distance it is--is an unhappy thing to reflect upon for anyone who knows how much remains to be done. We are like mountain-climbers in unexplored territory, who, at great cost, gain one peak, only to discover that it is merely a shoulder to another, distant, higher, and more formidable range.
>
> But as we sit here catching our breath and enjoying the newly revealed views and the sensation of having arrived, we are--as are all true mountain-climbers--compelled by those higher peaks and by the uneasy realization that even they may not be the last. Librarianship is one profession that has not found all the answers. Some of us wonder if it has found any.
>
> As I see it, it is the task of those of us now in office to be occupied with the first level of immediate problems: those of relating the tools and services of each of our libraries to the Center and to the other libraries in the new entity--a group of strong universities trying to become stronger through unity. These problems are well known to all of us who have been wrestling with them during the last decade.
>
> The first and, I suppose, the most stubborn is that of enlarging our sense of professional loyalties from a one-institution basis to a base that causes us to think first and always of the needs of each scholar in the region. This sounds easy and slightly un-American, but I can assure you that it is neither. At the moment, our universities are headed by a group of presidents who are intelligently determined to put intellectualism back into our universities. The least that is expected of us, as librarians, would be, it seems to me, some evidence, in the form of good

works, that librarians are interested in the welfare
of scholarship in this area. We can provide this
evidence by creating an abundance of the records
of scholarship by means of this Center. And how
do you go about the task of enlarging the members'
loyalties? By giving them practice in participation.

The second immediate task facing us is that of
reasoning with our faculties and helping them understand the necessity of this Center. This is a very
large order, and it is about all that the present
generation of librarians will have time to do. As
Mr. Metcalf has said, scholars of two generations
ago usually had to wait for years until they could
make the trip to Europe to consult the sources. Today our Center can make it possible for us to short-
en this delay to a day or two, but that will not im-
press the faculty member who has forgotten his predecessor's predicaments and is in no mood to be
reasonable about this Center, which to him appears
to be another whim of librarians to keep him from
his books. This would seem to be our opportunity.
May we be granted patience, eloquence, and thick
calluses where needed.

The third project we can and should tackle at
once is that of building a substantial book budget
with which to purchase new titles and which will
contribute to the research resources of the area.
Cooperative storage of publications is not the main
purpose of this association. Cooperative acquisition
and planning are.

Already we can see the benefits of cooperative
acquisition. The Center is about to enter microfilm subscriptions to forty foreign newspapers.
This will enable each of us to discard back files
of these papers. No one of us can afford to purchase all the patent reports published each year,
even though these are needed. But we can afford
to purchase a microcard file in the Center for all
of us. These are minor illustrations of the principle. But we shall not be able to supply the principles unless our points of view coincide and unless
our faculties approve.

Fourth, we should begin at once to survey the
special collection resources of the region and to
strengthen each existing special collection, whatever
it is, by gathering up the scattered fragments that
each of us may possess and concentrating these in

one place to make a single strong research resource. Each of us now possesses one or more of such collections, so the problem of undue concentration in one library will not prove to be a handicap.

Fifth, once we have solved these four problems, we can try to develop special services at the Center that can be offered more economically there than in individual libraries. Translating, central processing, microcopying, and publishing are examples of the type of services I mean.

These are a few of the tasks we have at hand-- primarily matters of relating the tools and services of each of our libraries to the Center and to the other libraries in the region. But shortly it will be clear to all that these rather minor matters will be overshadowed by others arising out of the relationships among this and similar centers in other parts of the country and between all the centers and the Library of Congress. We see already that this second level of library problems is immensely more complex than the one we now occupy, and we are eager to reach it.

For example, it is obvious now that we are nearing the end of the present system of individually compiled library catalogs. The traditional problems involved in getting from where we are to where we can use the Library of Congress printed catalogs-- author, title and subject--in an economical relationship to our local records are now slightly beyond our grasp. We must also find out how the relationships between each university library and regional centers and the Library of Congress can be affected by the use of teletype and other automatic machinery for sorting, counting, copying, and transporting books within the region and among the several regions.

The scope of these problems is national, and yet each must be analyzed and evaluated by the simple and undramatic test of what it means to the intellectual welfare of the solitary scholar. The fact that we can make early attacks on these problems means that we are in the first stages of developing a national system of library service for the twentieth-century scholar.

We librarians know that we must not make the mistake of trying to solve the library problems in our region on a regional basis alone. Each must

be evaluated in its national as well as regional setting. We resent this fact, but we shall not be able
to escape it.

I am aware that, once we have solved our local,
regional, and national problems, we shall merely
have laid the groundwork for the international ones
that lie ahead, but they can be postponed a while.
When these are finally solved, there will probably
be nothing more to do, but let us not be too sure.
In the meanwhile, while we gaze at the stars, it
is well for us to remember that we have a little
work to do here in the Midwest.

A grant from the Carnegie and Rockefeller Foundations
provided funds for the building and the construction began.

The difficulties the Executive Board had with Snead and
Company in constructing Macdonald's compact stack system at
the Center have been well covered by C. H. Bauman's Influence of Angus Macdonald and the Snead Bookstack on Library
Architecture (Scarecrow, 1967). This was a most unfortunate
episode for the MILC and for Mr. Macdonald. In my judgment it would not have happened if Mr. Macdonald had not
lost his manufacturing plant in Orange, Virginia. Snead and
Company came out of World War II in good shape for a new,
efficient factory and a strong staff. Macdonald's innovative
and restless mind led him into several kinds of experimen-
tation, for example, a prefabricated modular plank for wall
construction (this was used in the Bell Telephone Laboratories,
in Murray Hill, New Jersey) and the modular mock-up for
library construction, among others. To finance these he
stretched his credit too far and thus provided the opportunity
for the company that wanted his plant to persuade the local
banks to call in his loans at a time when he couldn't cover
them. After a long court battle Macdonald won the case, but
he never recovered his plant or his resources--one of the
really strange quirks in American court settlements.

The problem at MILC was that Macdonald had great
difficulty in getting the steel with which to fabricate the MILC
stacks, and then there was trouble between him and the con-
tractor over who was responsible for some unevenness in the
level of the floors, which had to be true to accommodate the
movable bookstacks. Ralph Esterquest was caught in the middle. In a letter to the Board, Mr. Esterquest referred to
some casters as substandard. This hurt Mr. Macdonald's
pride and led eventually to a law suit he brought against the

Center. This finally went to arbitration and was settled in Mr. Macdonald's favor.

At one point in the struggle, Mr. Middlebrook from the University of Minnesota and I (a subcommittee on the building problem) were called to Chicago to meet with Mr. Macdonald to see if we could authorize advance payment to Mr. Macdonald for part of his work. His financial state at that time was evidenced by the fact that he let us pay for the luncheon--something that most generous and hospitable gentleman must have hated bitterly. Mr. Middlebrook and I agreed, after consulting our attorney, that we had no authority to make the advance. To his dying day Mr. Macdonald felt that I had let him down by not favoring the advance. After all, we had had long and close personal associations in developing the modular method. I very much regretted the fact that it was not legally possible to approve the advance.

The financial losses Mr. Macdonald incurred in the MILC project were probably responsible for his inability to regather the kind of staff he had always had, and to recover his position in the library bookstack business. This was a great loss to the library profession. His creative imagination and innovative spirit were to be missed at a time when they were needed.

I would be less than frank if I didn't admit that I am highly pleased with the way in which the Center has evolved into the kind of institution I always thought, during the early stages, it could become.

The Cooperative Committee on Large University Library Building Planning

In 1944-45, Julian Boyd of Princeton and John Burchard of M. I. T. led in the organizing of the librarians and architects of some seventeen universities that were planning post-war library buildings. The group met several times a year on the member campuses. The results of the Committee's work can be found in the book, Planning University Library Buildings (1949), by Burchard, Boyd and David, and in the published Minutes of the various meetings of the Cooperative Committee.

But the real importance was the rapport developed

within our group, which permitted honest and informed crit-
icisms of each other's plans.   Each of us had visited the
campuses and studied the setting of the building as well as
its blueprints to the point where we had a real understanding
of the project.   This is in great contrast to the present-day
A. L. A. Pre-Conference Building Institutes, which with their
hundreds of attendees serve as a marketplace for consultants
and where speakers can bolster their egos by displaying their
expertise.   But these critics have not had the intimate contact they should have had before they attempt to evaluate an
institution's plans.   And, as one participant said, "They tell
you the things you already know, and never tell you what you
need to know. "   I eschew such meetings.

Aside from participating in all the sessions, my only
important contribution to the group was informing Julian Boyd,
then chairman, about the modular mock-up Angus Macdonald
had constructed in Orange, New Jersey, to demonstrate how
libraries could use modular planning.   As a result of my telephone call, Mr. Boyd visited the mock-up and then arranged
to have the fall meeting of the Coop Committee in the mock-
up.   This meeting was an important step in the development
of modular planning.

In the spirit of his usual hospitality and generosity,
Mr. Macdonald had arranged for our group to do a tour of
Virginia's famous Skyline Drive, ending with a cookout on the
Rapidan at President Hoover's "Camp David. "   We were
served large mint juleps and fried chicken, and were entertained by a local group of black singers.   One of the architects from Rice University drank a few too many juleps, which
freed him of his inhibitions, and during the evening he took
me aside and told me in no uncertain terms how stupid modular planning was and how I should be ashamed of my part in
promoting it.   Many years later I had the pleasure of trying
to help Rice University figure out how to remodel and enlarge
that architect's building--a nearly impossible task because the
building was so inflexible.

At another session, on the Princeton campus, the University had arranged a kind of mock-up in an old building in
which there were various kinds of light fixtures, and in which
the ceiling could be raised and lowered, so we could decide
on what should be the minimum floor-to-ceiling dimension.
General consensus was that 8 feet 6 inches was the minimum,
and that became gospel.   At one point, Charlie David of Pennsylvania wondered why the people on the other side of the

room looked better than the ones on his (referring, of course, to the light fixtures), to which someone on the other side replied that they were better people.

One of our meetings was scheduled at Duke University in Durham, and we all arranged to take an overnight train from Washington, D.C. I had been working at Orange, Virginia (eighty miles southwest of Washington) with Mr. Macdonald, and had arranged to get on the train at Orange about midnight. The porter informed me that there had been a mixup and that someone was in my berth. I insisted that the person be put out. After a short wait I was told my berth was ready, and I went to sleep. The next morning at breakfast Mr. L. C. O'Connor, that tall and dignified architect from the firm of Kilham and O'Connor, which was doing the Firestone Library at Princeton, came in complaining of having been put out of his berth in the middle of the night. I blanch in recollection.

The Dissertation Abstracts Project

One of the gaps in the distribution of the literature of scholarship opened up about the time of World War II because by then most American universities had stopped requiring graduate students to publish their dissertations in book form. They were availabe only on interlibrary loan. European universities, however, continued the old practices and their dissertations continued to arrive on an exchange basis. Many wanted something in return. Also, although some of the information in the best of our dissertations eventually found its way into the stream of scholarship, in the form of journal articles and even printed books, much valuable information was lost; and even when the dissertation information became available the delay was always long.

The Association of Research Libraries created a committee, of which I was chairman, to study this gap and to find ways of closing it. Naturally, we turned to microfilming as the best solution. There was already an ongoing publishing project through whose service we thought we could publish our dissertations. I refer to the "Microfilm Abstracts" publication program run by University Microfilms, Inc. The essence of their program was publishing the theses and dissertation abstracts in "Microfilm Abstracts," and the making of positives of the dissertations for sale upon demand.

This program seemed appropriate for expansion at the national and international level. I began discussions with Eugene Power, then president of University Microfilms, Inc. There was a sharp difference of opinion within the committee (later reflected in ARL), not about the nature of the program but over who should control it. One member wanted the Library of Congress to do it; one member objected to having a commercial company control it. My point of view was that the service would have to be fast and accurate and responsive to changing demand and I did not see that the Library of Congress at that time could be sure of meeting those conditions. As a devout New Deal Democrat I believed that one should use the private business sector as long as it could deliver the goods, efficiently, promptly and at a reasonable price--which of course included the possibility of making a reasonable profit. Besides, since University Microfilms, Inc. had developed the plan, it seemed ungracious, if not illegal, to propose to take the program away from them. It also seemed wrong to use tax-free university laboratories to compete on equal terms with commercial laboratories that had to pay taxes and also to make a profit.

The final program the committee brought for approval to the 1951 annual session of the Association of Research Libraries, meeting in Iowa City, insisted that there be only one publication in which dissertation abstracts would be published, and that University Microfilms, Inc. should manage it. Dissertations would be mailed by the sponsoring university to Ann Arbor, where they would be microfilmed by University Microfilms, Inc., thus guaranteeing high quality. Positives of the dissertations would be sold by University Microfilms, Inc., but authors could, if they wished, publish the dissertations later as books or journal articles. The film negatives would be considered as the archival copy and would be kept in the vaults of University Microfilms, Inc.

One of the reasons why we wanted University Microfilms to manage the projects was that they were in a position to make the financial investment in storage vaults, filming equipment and personnel that would be constantly expanding, whereas we couldn't be sure that a university or the Library of Congress would have access to the money when it would be needed.

Discussion at the Iowa City 1951 sessions of ARL was heated and bitter. I was accused on the floor of the meeting of having accepted bribes from University Microfilms, Inc., or at least of being in their secret employment. Arguments were put forward for placing the service at the Library of Congress or in a university photo laboratory. Our reply to the charge that a commercial company like University Microfilms could take advantage of the participating universities was two-fold: one, that it would not be to their advantage to do so; and two, that ARL could stop using the service and set up its own any time it wanted to.

But, as I said, the plan was bitterly debated and feelings ran high. Finally the meeting adjourned at 4:30 and the members boarded university buses to go to my house for cocktails.

Our neighbors, for years after, loved to tell about some fifty rather tall men stalking out of the buses and into our house, wordless. Professor Stow Persons, who served as barman, told me later that the group consumed an average of four martinis apiece. The noise level rose to the point where the immediate neighbors became concerned, and I glanced out the windows, nervously looking for the cops.

Finally, after an hour or so of drinking, all the members but one rolled out of the house into the bus: everyone by that time was in a jovial and rosy mood. Our neighbors noticed the difference and marveled greatly.

The Chairman called for a vote on the committee plan first thing in the evening session and the plan was approved with no dissent, thus reaffirming the value of the martini to civilize the human beast. The one member who chose to walk to the dinner, rather than ride the bus, never made it. I think he decided to take a nap in a ditch between our house and the dormitory. He was all right the next day, but slightly subdued.

The committee had much work to do during the next five years in working with Eugene Power and Stevens Rice of University Microfilms, Inc. to solve the problems that arose. One of the hardest problems was to get the participating universities to send in the dissertations and abstracts for filming on time. John Cronin was extremely helpful in working out details for the cataloging of the dissertations according to Library of Congress standards.

The program expanded rapidly until today almost all American universities participate, as do many foreign universities.

Centralized Cataloging

I don't remember when it dawned on me that our national cataloging economy seemed absurd. As late as 1940, most university libraries maintained a staff of professional catalogers at
work describing the contents of each incoming book as though
it were the only library cataloging the book. They did this
even though a so-called system of Cooperative Cataloging did
exist, with the Library of Congress as the nerve center.
Most universities purchased Library of Congress catalog cards
all right, but most catalogers felt, as a matter of principle,
that they should make as many changes in the cards as possible. This seemed pretty wasteful of valuable talent.

At any rate, in 1945 I published what seemed like a
Rube Goldberg plan for complete centralized cataloging, under
the title "Centralized Cataloging for Scholarly Libraries."
The following portion of the plan summarized the two aspects:
identification cataloging and bibliographical operations.

I. IDENTIFICATION CATALOGING

1. There would be a new recording device, consisting of a location symbol card (referred to hereafter
as l. s. c.) upon which are printed 1,120 numbers,
each representing a library. Not more than a thousand numbers would be assigned at first.
2. The Library of Congress Union Catalog staff
would file an l. s. c. after the main entry for all
books now listed and then record the holdings of
the thousand participating libraries, adding new l.
s. c.'s for new entries as they appear and checking
ownership for each on the l. s. c.'s.
3. When the holdings of the thousand libraries
were recorded, the Library of Congress Union Catalog would consist of all the titles owned by the
thousand largest scholarly libraries, with ownership indicated for each title in all thousand libraries.
4. The Library of Congress would then publish
the catalog, each l. s. c. following its entry card,
in format similar to the Library of Congress Catalog of Printed Cards (unless a better technique is
developed). This would be called the basic catalog.
5. After printing the basic catalog, the Library
of Congress would continue to record in it the new
holdings reported by libraries and would keep a
separate additions catalog of new titles (those copy-

righted within the year) added by the thousand libraries, printing this at the end of the year.   Entries for each succeeding year would be interfiled
in the additions catalog, and this would be printed
each year for twenty years.   At the end of each
twenty years, the additions catalog cards would be
interfiled with the basic catalog and a new basic
catalog printed.   All back issues of the printed catalog would be discarded.

6.   Each of the thousand libraries would buy the
basic and additions catalog and would keep a card
catalog of the books added during the year following the last edition of the additions catalog--but only
the ones published during the year.   Older titles
added would be checked in the basic additions catalogs.

7.   Merritt estimated in 1942 that there were
then some 9, 800, 000 titles in American libraries.
Assuming this to be true, the first edition of the
basic catalog might contain eleven million entries,
or twenty-two million, including the l. s. c. 's.   The
Library of Congress Catalog of Printed Cards contains 11, 520 entries per volume.   Thus, for twenty-
two million entries, a catalog of some nineteen hundred volumes is indicated.   This would occupy about
260 linear feet of shelving.

8.   On the basis of the Library of Congress Catalog of Printed Cards, which cost $600 for 160 vol-
umes, or roughly $4. 00 per volume, the proposed
basic catalog would cost about $7, 600.   But there
were only 500 copies of the Library of Congress
Catalog printed, and there would be at least 2, 500
copies of the proposed catalog printed.   Some libraries would want more than one copy;   and some
nonparticipating libraries, especially foreign libraries, would buy copies.   Thus, the cost per volume
should be somewhat lower.   The whole problem of
cost would have to be worked out.

Estimates of the number of new titles published
each year that are added to the thousand libraries
are not available.   Five hundred thousand would be
an exceedingly inclusive guess.   The actual figures
would probably be much smaller.   Half a million
entries plus an equal number of l. s. c. 's would fill
about 85 volumes, which at Library of Congress
Catalog rates would be $340.   But, since 3, 000
copies of the additions catalog would be needed, the

cost might be expected to be lower. Presumably, many nonparticipating libraries would use this tool.

Thus, the basic catalog might cost $7,600, and the annual additions catalog $340 or less.

II. SUBJECT BIBLIOGRAPHIC APPARATUS

1. There would be two printed subject bibliography services for each of the thirty-eight major subject fields. (These represent the subject fields now included in the largest American university; the figure is subject to revision, depending on how the definitions are drawn.) These services would be compiled and printed under the auspices of a bibliographic institute. One service would be for the undergraduate. It would list a few books and articles as introductions to the subject and a few books to be used in learning the tool subjects that must be understood before the subject itself can be approached. It would also list a number of titles that show the relations of the subject to related fields. And it would, of course, cover the subdivisions of the subject. The list would be highly selective and carefully annotated. It would be a tool for the young learner. One or two cumulated editions a year would probably be sufficient.

The second tool would be for the advanced student and the researcher. It would be a scholar's bibliography and would list all references that are relevant. It would be based upon and coordinated with existing bibliographic tools in the subject.

2. Both services or tools would be printed in cumulative form. Out-of-date and irrelevant entries would be dropped from each new issue. The compilation and editorial work would be done by librarians with specialized knowledge of the subject field concerned. They would work under the direction of a distinguished subject specialist.

3. All thirty-eight institutes could be located at the Library of Congress or each could be located at the university or special library having the largest collection and the most distinguished group of associated scholars in the field.

4. Each service would cost $15 per year, or $1,140 for all seventy-six.

5. The entire subject-bibliography project would be under the direction of a council appointed by the

American Council of Learned Societies. Each institute would work closely with the learned or professional society concerned.

Although many parts of the scheme now seem fantas-
tic, other parts have become a reality, thanks to the computer (which really became a mechanical substitute for the
manual location card idea), and to the leadership of Frederick Kilgour, John Cronin, William Welsh, and the many others at the Library of Congress who got the MARC project
onto a going basis. The plan had some good ideas which
couldn't be put into practice until the right machines were
perfected.

Two other statements may have had some influence on
the development of centralized cataloging. One is by Norman
Kilpatrick and myself called, "The Midwest Reaches for the
Stars" (College and Research Libraries, April 1948, pages
1-9). This article outlined two possibilities for a regional
attack on the problem. To disarm those who might consider
us completely crazy, we offered the following warning in our
introduction:

> We are aware that there is a kind of psycholog-
> ical disorder which causes a man who cannot solve
> his personal problems to turn to grandiose schemes
> which are nearly perfect in themselves, but which
> lack a few connecting links with reality, and the
> lack destroys the validity. It is often difficult to
> distinguish, at any given time, between the efforts
> of a man whose toes, all ten of them, are up in
> the clouds, and one who has his feet solidly on the
> ground.

The plan won no converts, not even in the Midwest
Inter-Library Center group, for which it was written; yet it
did (at least so he said) lead Luther Evans to invite me to
spend a month at the Library of Congress as Visiting Chief
of the Union Catalog Division for the month of October 1948.
My report to Dr. Evans was published in an appendix to the
Library of Congress Information Bulletin (November 1948,
pages 16-22). The sky didn't fall, but neither did a cataloging revolution begin as a result of my report, which was the
second of the two reports I referred to earlier.

Feeling frustrated because nothing I wrote was causing
any real action on the centralized cataloging front, I wrote an

editorial blast that first appeared in the <u>Colorado Academic Librarian</u>:

> The matter of timing is usually the crucial fac-
> tor in determing the rate of progress an educational
> institution maintains. This is certainly true of li-
> braries, particularly college and university libraries.
> And timing frequently turns out to be a matter of
> people--specific individuals.
>
> For example, when the Honorable Archibald Mac-
> Leish took a look at the salaries the Library of
> Congress was paying in the 1930s, he is reported
> to have been shocked. He soon was able to raise
> the rates considerably. His actions immediately
> shook the complacency of library administrators all
> over the country and from that time, librarians'
> salaries all over the country began to rise. Ten
> years earlier, or later, Mr. MacLeish might not
> have been able to work his magic.
>
> Likewise, when Dr. Paul Buck became director
> of Libraries at Harvard, his statesmanlike policy
> and action on the academic status of professional
> librarians marked a major turning point on this is-
> sue and put an end to the influence of the management-
> minded administrators who had succeeded in many
> universities--such as UCLA and University of Cali-
> fornia--in putting professional librarians on the non-
> academic side of the fence.
>
> I think another such time for action is coming up
> this year on the question of Centralized Cataloging.
>
> In spite of the fact that for more than 50 years
> there have been librarians who understood clearly
> the need for Centralized Cataloging, in spite of
> everything the Library of Congress has done, in
> spite of our so-called cooperative cataloging plan,
> in spite of the life work of John Cronin and George
> Schwegmann, Jr., in spite of some directors of li-
> braries and some catalogers who could distinguish
> between the economy of cataloging and the act of
> cataloging, we still have precious little centralized
> cataloging, nor is what we have extensive enough
> to enable libraries to reduce their cataloging costs
> or change their staffing patterns.
>
> Visit the university libraries of the country and
> go into the technical processes rooms and you will
> see the same thing everywhere: scores of able, but
> harassed catalogers surrounded by piles of books and

journals written in languages the catalogers don't read easily and by books being held for Library of Congress cards.

Call on the directors of these libraries and you will find men who really think they can employ enough catalogers to catalog these books--at a cost of three to six dollars, catalogers who can read the the languages of Eastern Europe, the Near and Far East and of Africa. You will find men who know that holding new books for printed Library of Congress cards means weeks of delay in getting books into the hands of readers.

But you will not find men who are so aware of the absolute futility of going on with our existing economy of cataloging that they are willing to take the steps that must be taken to bring full Centralized Cataloging into being. You will not find men who can accept the idea that their big cataloging room should be almost empty, or that a large part of their cataloging budget should go to Washington. You will not find men who are willing to get off their chairs and fight for Centralized Cataloging.

The Library of Congress officers know what should be done--John Cronin, George Schwegmann, Jr., Richard Angell, Rudy Rogers, Quincy Mumford, and others less directly involved. Verner Clapp, when he was Assistant Librarian of Congress, understood the issue. But the Library of Congress men dare not put themselves in the position of imposing a system of centralized cataloging on the country. They have had to wait for us librarians to ask. And we have not asked!

Personally, through my writing, speeches and my terms as chairman of the ALA Committee on Resources, I have done everything I could to persuade my colleagues to act. But, essentially I got nowhere. And Gordon Williams, now Chairman, is trying, too. (Mr. Williams did get the P. L. 480 Centralized Cataloging project started--a major accomplishment.) Library directors simply don't think the situation is that serious or that the problems can be licked, or that they can overcome staff resistance in their own libraries.

Yes, much has been done. The National Union Catalog at its present state of development is monumental. A library like ours at the University of Colorado can purchase centralized cataloging infor-

mation for some 60 per cent of the books it acquires
--but not quickly enough. The Cataloging in Source
project made sense for a limited aspect of the problem. John Cronin's Cards-with-Books program,
too, will help. Cooperative cataloging as it is
practiced is too slow to be useful and too limited
in scope and concept to satisfy the requirements
for Centralized Cataloging. The P. L. 480 Centralized Cataloging project is impressive but limited to
two geographic areas.

I think there are four reasons why some directors of libraries are sitting on their hands instead
of acting on Centralized Cataloging: first, they
aren't interested and they don't realize how much
money they are wasting or how much slow and low
quality cataloging service they offer their readers;
second, they are scared stiff over all the hard work
that would be involved in shifting dollars and staff
to a centralized cataloging agency; third, they think
automation and computers will solve the problem;
and fourth, they know that full Centralized Cataloging would force them to face up to the necessity of
reconciling the new system with their own catalog,
full of a whole manual of local rules and adaptations.

Let us be clear about two points:

(1) The act of doing the original cataloging for
a book is an important, complex, creative and interesting act. Original cataloging should be done
carefully, fully, and all necessary secondary entries
and subject headings should be made--not just three,
but twenty, if necessary. The amount of time required or the dollars spent are unimportant. But
this work should never be done more than once.
Thus, it is our cataloging economy that is at fault,
not the individual cataloger.

(2) Half-way tools or services do not help very
much. Centralized Cataloging must be so compre-
hensive and inclusive that it enables libraries like
ours to stop doing most of the cataloging we are
now doing. Otherwise, the tools and services are
nothing more than desirable luxuries.

Next year will be crucial. The Association of
Research Libraries has now enlarged its membership, has incorporated, has a very wise, energetic
resourceful and knowledgeable executive secretary
in the person of Dr. James Skipper.

It is my hope and guess, and I speak without

authorization from anyone, that A. R. L. will propose the establishment of a National Cataloging Center in Washington, in rented space, and that it will
begin by doing the contract cataloging for books from
countries with the less common languages--from the
Near and Far East, Africa and some of the East
European languages.

Each library ordering books from these countries
could have then sent to the National Cataloging Center (the number of errors in filling orders is not
large enough to become a barrier) which would catalog the books and send them, along with the cards
to the library that ordered them. Each library
would be billed for services rendered on a unit cost
basis.

If A. R. L. would do this, the Library of Congress
could concentrate on providing rapid cataloging copy
for books in English and the more common European
languages. It, too, could contract with the A. R. L.
for cataloging service for the unusual language
books.

How would A. R. L. finance this operation? By
charging libraries for the work it does for them.

Where will A. R. L. get catalogers to do the work?
From the staffs of our libraries. If A. R. L. and
the Library of Congress really take this problem
seriously, and set up a full service, each of our
staffs can be reduced, eventually, to the point where
we need only enough professionals to do local imprints and adjustment work. This means that many
of our catalogers would move to Washington. Those
who don't choose to do so can be moved to other
vacancies within each library, or to other libraries
that are unwilling or unable to solve their local
cataloging problems completely enough to take advantage of Centralized Cataloging. There are, we
are told, 25,000 unfilled professional library positions in the United States.

Why should A. R. L. rather than the Library of
Congress offer this service? The Library of Congress has never been able in recent times to get
a large enough appropriation to enlarge its buildings or its staff sufficiently and promptly enough
to keep up with the demand for Centralized Cataloging. Furthermore, the question of the national
library status of the Library of Congress has never
been clarified fully and directly. Centralized Cata-

loging is too important and complicated a problem
to be left on the present indefinite basis. The A.
R. L. 's income for Centralized Cataloging can enlarge immediately and to the extent needed to meet
the requirements of its members. It can rent space
in Washington. Each library participating in the
services of the National Cataloging Center would
know that its cataloging costs would depend on the
amount of material it sent to the Center for cataloging. Once unit costs are developed, there could
be no question of how much each library pays. Nor
would the Center need to worry about income. Each
year it would be able to estimate the volume of work
it would be expected to do and it could adjust the
size of its staff and space accordingly. The Library
of Congress cannot possibly have this flexibility.

Would this be an additional cost to libraries?
No. If it were, the whole idea would be no good.
This is the crux of the problem. It would be a
substitute for cataloging cost that would otherwise
exist in each library. Thus far, with the exception
of one or two specific projects, Centralized Cataloging has failed to go far enough to enable specific
libraries to change their cataloging staff and cost
patterns. We are now in a position to go far enough.

But, can libraries carry out their responsibilities
locally so that they can take full advantage of Centralized Cataloging? Some will and some won't try,
mostly because they fail to comprehend the issues
involved. There is no real reason why a library cannot make the necessary adjustments. In some libraries automation is relevant and in some, not.
The timing of the A. L. A. catalog code revision is
involved. My guess is that libraries will print their
pre-revised code catalogs and throw away their old
card catalogs, starting a new catalog based on computer stored records.

When will A. R. L. start the Centralized Cataloging Center? I have no authority to speak for A. R.
L. I do not know how long it would take 65 heads
of large university libraries to come to the realization that A. R. L. can and should establish this Center. My guess is that the decision will come quickly and that two years will be needed to get the Center into operation.

If we don't do this, there is no way of avoiding
a cataloging crisis the size of which will be so great

that university presidents will be completely justified in asking why their library directors failed to
take action sooner.

My suggestion of setting up a separate agency in Washington was made with full malice of forethought. I hoped it
would have the effect of moving the profession toward the
Library of Congress.

From that time on there was a confluence of many
influences, and I am no judge of how much my writings
helped, or hindered. Perhaps William Dix's summary is the
best balanced account of the developments after 1948:

* * *

"Perhaps the first event to have a direct connection with the
present development was the publication in 1948 of an informal and personal set of proposals by Ralph E. Ellsworth,
then Director of Libraries at the State University of Iowa,
following a one-month stay at the Library of Congress as
Visiting Chief of the Union Catalog Division. Ellsworth
stated boldly and flatly, 'I have come to the conclusion that
L. C. can and should inaugurate a program of Centralized
Cataloging as defined in this report, and that it can do so
without undue hardship to its internal affairs and its financial
resources'; he then went on to detail his proposals.

"Nothing happened immediately, but discussion continued,
ued, and at the Forty-eighth Meeting of the Association of
Research Libraries on January 18, 1957, Louis Kaplan presented a proposal signed by himself and Ellsworth calling for
a thorough study of cooperative cataloging by a new ARL
committee. Jens Nyholm objected to limiting the inquiry to
cooperative cataloging and submitted a document advocating
a study of centralized cataloging as well, with particular reference to current foreign imprints received through the Farm-
ington Plan. The members voted that a committee should be
established, to consider both cooperative and centralized cataloging, and then went on to discuss financial arrangements for
the proposed study.

"About the same time John M. Dawson published, in
the January 1957 issue of Library Quarterly, 'The Acquisitions and Cataloging of Research Libraries: a Study of the
Possibilities for Centralized Processing,' a careful examination of the procedures and experience of nine sample uni-

versity libraries in using LC cards. This important article helped keep interest in the issue alive, yet the ARL committee found itself unable to obtain the funds required for the thorough analysis of the problem which it proposed.

"The urge to attack the problem once again was felt by Richard M. Logsdon, Director of Libraries at Columbia University. As Chairman of the ARL he wrote to Ellsworth on October 23, 1963, 'What are you doing on the cooperative cataloging business? I could make good use of an immediate answer ...' and again on October 19, 'Since writing to you a few days ago I have pretty much come to the conclusion that ARL could do nothing more important in the next year or two than to improve the situation with respect to coordinated and centralized cataloging.' Ellsworth replied characteristically on November 7, 'Well, at least someone else realizes that the centralized cataloging problem has got to be solved! Hurrah!'

"Ellsworth had independently renewed his own attack on the problem in a forceful editorial written in the summer of 1963 for the fall issue of a new journal, The Colorado Academic Library, published by the College and University Section of the Colorado Library Association. He suggested that the Association of Research Libraries might establish in Washington, outside the Library of Congress, a National Cataloging Center to begin by doing contract cataloging for books from countries with the less common languages, with each participating library billed for services rendered on a unit cost basis. On December 16, 1963, he sent a copy of this editorial to the director of each ARL library, with a covering letter saying:

> I take it that editorials are usually written for the purpose of stimulating thought or action or both.
> I will admit that my argument for establishing a National Cataloging Foundation outside the Library of Congress was advanced with malice of forethought. If L. C. can control the factors that are essential to a sensible national economy of cataloging, my argument is unnecessary. But if L. C. cannot do this, and it has not done so in the past, then my argument is valid.
> The real question is whether L. C., financed and controlled as it is by Congress, can meet the present needs of large libraries.
> I hope the editorial puts the question in a way that will lead to its solution.

"Logsdon, in November, began making plans with James
E. Skipper, Executive Secretary of the ARL, collecting data
and drafting a resolution to be presented to the Board of Directors:

> Resolved that in view of:
> (1) The substantial costs of cataloging in research
>   libraries (approximately 16% of total library
>   operating expenditures),
> (2) The rising percentage of original cataloging
>   that is now necessary (forty-seven libraries
>   report an average of 46% original cataloging
>   required in 1963),
> (3) Increasing arrearages of uncataloged materials
>   (the same reporting libraries indicate that their
>   arrearage has increased an average of 160%
>   during the past ten years),
> That the Association of Research Libraries should
> give the highest priority during the next few years
> to developing a program for decreasing the amount
> of original cataloging, working in conjunction with
> representatives of the Library of Congress and oth-
> er library groups.   Specifically, this will include a
> study of the Library of Congress proposal of Janu-
> ary 7, 1964, which is a result of the thinking of
> its staff in response to a request from the ALA
> Committee on Resources, Subcommittee on the Na-
> tional Union Catalog;
> That the Board shall report to the members at
> the St. Louis Meeting concerning these efforts.
> This resolution recognizes the significance of the
> issue and the complexity of the problems involved.

"The Library of Congress draft proposal, not discussed
at the meeting, but referred to the new committee by the resolution, was printed as an appendix to the minutes of the
meeting.   It offered two alternative plans for achieving an
improvement in the amount of available Library of Congress
cataloging copy.   One plan involved the provision locally by
cooperating libraries of National Union Catalog copy for all
post-1956 non-U. S. titles acquired by them and the distribution of this copy by the Library of Congress to other libraries
requiring it.   The other tentative plan involved the production
and distribution centrally by the Library of Congress of stand-
ardized entries for post-1956 non-U. S. titles, borrowing from
other libraries for cataloging purposes volumes not acquired
by the Library of Congress.

"It is obvious that the thought and discussion which went into the preparation of this memorandum under the direction of John Cronin helped prepare the way for the evolution of the plan which was to emerge and for its commendably rapid implementation by the Library of Congress. It should be noted, however, that there are significant differences: it was not intended that the Library of Congress increase its acquisitions of foreign books substantially for cataloging purposes; no mechanism was provided, other than the printed National Union Catalog and proof sheets, for prompt determination of availability and need; and the question of funding the operation was left unresolved: 'It is quite certain that Congress would not appropriate the funds required to catalog titles not held by the Library of Congress and it would be necessary for the research libraries to supply the needed money.'

"Soon after the meeting the following accepted appointment by the Chairman of the ARL to the committee called for in the resolution: Ralph E. Ellsworth, University of Colorado; Richard H. Logsdon, Columbia University; Stephen A. McCarthy, Cornell University; James E. Skipper, Executive Secretary, ARL; William S. Dix, Princeton University, Chairman.

"Somewhat later Edmon Low, Oklahoma State University, accepted appointment. At its first meeting it decided to identify itself as the ARL Shared Cataloging Committee, thus avoiding the premature decision between cooperative and centralized cataloging.

"Without attempting to recapitulate the discussions and conclusions of each of the many meetings which followed or the reports made at each of the semi-annual meetings of the ARL, it can be seen in retrospect that the discussions and activities of the Committee, of the Librarian of Congress and his staff, and of others who became involved were marked by a series of identifiable decisions."

* * *

Ironically, even though I meant just the opposite when in my editorial I suggested a separate cataloging agency, that is, in fact, what has happened in part with the creation of the Ohio College Library Center and the Research Libraries' Information Network (R. L. I. N.), although the Library of Congress is still the heart of the networks. Which proves, as any trout angler knows, "that you can't hardly find any water anymore where you can be sure of the kind of fish you are going to catch."

The American Right Wing Collection Project

It has always seemed strange to me that while university librarians have always busied themselves gathering as many published works of their time as possible, few have bothered to collect the primary source material of groups and individuals who were important in shaping public opinion, or cultural innovations of their time. For example, did Oxford University collect anything that would be helpful to us today in knowing all about Shakespeare's life and times?

I thought it would be a good idea to start some of that kind of collecting in the University of Iowa Library. I was aware that the University of Wisconsin was collecting source material about the left wing groups in America, but no one seemed interested in the right wing. I'm not sure why I thought the right wingers would be worth collecting, or that they would become important. Maybe I had in my brain the kind of magnet Larry Powell used to talk about when he prowled through old second hand bookstores.

At any rate, I began what I first called the "Tensions File," i.e., source material from groups and individuals that expressed themselves in print about the obvious tension points in American society. Some of these tension points were: fluoridation, the federal income tax, the Alaska Mental Health Hospital bill, East Berlin, progressive education, states' rights, the Warren Supreme Court, foreign aid, labor unions and right to work laws, the Social Security system, federal aid to health and education, Communists in government, etc. I set aside a large room in the library and tried to spend a couple of hours each day writing to the groups and sorting the incoming mail by "tension points." I speculated that these groups would be sending their messages to their senators and consequently I visited Iowa's representatives in Washington and asked them to save their junk mail for me. They did and once a week sent a big mail bag along to us. This source proved to be a gold mine. Although I collected on all the "tension points," I soon found that the right wing groups were the most interesting and I concentrated on them. In writing to them I was careful to explain my neutral position and that it was important for the future history of the country

to have their beliefs preserved. They took me at my word
and freely sent their letters and bulletins.

I had the help of three highly intelligent faculty wives,
Mrs. Ruth Stout, Mrs. Lois Porter and Mrs. Sarah Harris.
The American Jewish Center and the Anti-Defamation League
were very helpful. They had been watching the right wing
groups, most of which were anti-semitic in doctrine, and knew
a great deal about them.

When it became obvious that we had a resource that
could have national significance, and when the incoming mail
became too large to take care of with Iowa's limited budget,
I sought financial aid from the Fund for the Republic to enlarge my collecting network and to process the material. I
suggested that in return for the grant I would write an annotated bibliography of the right wing groups. The Fund gave
us a small grant--$4, 500. 00, as I recall. Mrs. Harris, my
assistant, had a Ph. D. degree in English Literature and had
done considerable research for the University of Chicago his-
torian, Dr. Samuel Harper, and was a capable scholar in her
own right. By 1957-59, we felt we had a sufficiently compre-
hensive coverage of the right wing groups and individuals to
justify publishing the bibliography. Mrs. Harris and I worked
together on the organization of the report, and she wrote
most of the annotations, although I did some and worked
closely with her on all of them. We submitted a copy of the
report to the Fund, and I seem to remember a letter of
thanks from one of their officers.

Word of the bibliography got around and I was asked
by Dr. Harold Lancour of the University of Illinois Library
School if they could publish it in their Occasional Papers
series. Mrs. Harris was reluctant to have this done because
she felt the report needed corrections and revisions, which
she was unable to do because of a serious illness (she died
in the summer of 1958). Since I had left Iowa for Colorado
in January 1958 I saw no hope of being able to do the revised edition myself, and so I gave Illinois permission to
publish it (R. E. Ellsworth and Sarah M. Harris, The American Right Wing: a Report to the Fund for the Republic).

In 1961, Mr. Schnapper, President of the Public Affairs Press in Washington, telephoned me and asked if he
could republish the report and give it the wide circulation he
believed it deserved. He also wanted to bring it up to date,
but I explained that since I was separated from the sources

I couldn't do that. I said I would add a section in which I
would speculate on what the future of the right wing groups
might be. He agreed. I assumed he would seek permission
from the Fund and from Illinois for the republishing. It
turned out later that this apparently was not done. In fact,
neither publisher had asked the Fund's permission. I added
several pages to the Illinois edition.

I have never known how many copies of the report
were sold by the Public Affairs Press. I do recall that Steve
Allen wrote for several copies for his friends. I also recall
that James Bromley, one of the conservative Regents of the
University of Colorado, brought an unfavorable review of the
report to the attention of the Board of Regents and said I
should be fired. The Regents apparently didn't think I was
worth bothering about. At least they didn't try to fire me.

But in the December 22, 1961 issue of Science magazine (p. 46) there appeared a long critical editorial of the
report, written by a Howard Margolis, under the title, "Right
Wingers Seem to Be Almost Everywhere: Notes on a Report
to the Fund for the Republic."

In this review we were accused of everything from
drawing ridiculous relationships between Right Wingers and
moderate Republicans, to falsifying our relations to the Fund
for the Republic, even though the Fund Secretary told Mr.
Margolis that we had not done so. We had never claimed
that our report was a report of the Fund. The subtitle was
merely descriptive of what the report was, as a part of the
small grant we had received.

In common with most liberals of that period, apparently Mr. Margolis was unable to take seriously my prediction
that right wing groups would play an increasingly important
part in American politics. I was predicting. I had no proof,
of course, that my predictions would come true.

Even though our report contained minor mistakes,
caused by the fact that Mrs. Harris died before she had a
chance to correct them, we were exactly right in our basic
analysis of the influence of the groups. As of February 1979
the so-called conservative groups and individuals in the United
States hold economic, social, educational, financial and governmental views that are very close to those of the Right
Wingers of yesterday and today--the ones we were describing.
I suppose it was the following sentences I wrote that irritated
Mr. Margolis:

Ten years ago liberals, moderates and uncom-
mitted citizens could, and did, scoff at the Right
Wing as a 'fringe' group concerned in a crazy
manner with unimportant issues. What they failed
to understand, and what this report tries to clar-
ify, is the fact that in terms of basic economic,
political and governmental issues the Right Wing
held the same beliefs as did the moderate conservatives of both major parties. They differed only
in their concern with fringe issues, in their manner of speaking and in their sense of fair play.

The significance of recent developments is simply that in a time of deep crisis, the moderates
are more willing to go along with, and be carried
by, the extremists. (R. E. Ellsworth and Sarah
M. Harris, The American Right Wing: a Report
to the Fund for the Republic.)

Incidentally, we became embroiled in controversy with
the editor of U. S. News and World Report for calling it a
right wing magazine. What we should have said was that the
editorials written by Mr. Lawrence were right-wingish in
content.

Another repercussion from our report and from the
A. L. A. 75th anniversary celebration (which I shall explain
later) came in a column written by Russell Kirk in Buckley's
National Review. The editorial said in part:

For some years (on the Boulder campus of the
University of Colorado) a circle of the sort of in-
tolerant zealots whom Dr. Sidney Hook calls 'rit-
ualistic liberals'--if not persons still further toward the Left--has made life at Boulder unpleas-
ant for any student or professor who holds less
bigoted opinions. Probably the most conspicuous
of these illiberal 'liberals' is a certain Ralph Ellsworth. Mr. Ellsworth, an expert on the utilization
of library space, earlier this year endeavored to
establish himself as an expert on the 'American
Right Wing' and published a booklet by that title,
distributed by a vanity press. Though Mr. Ellsworth subtitled his diatribe 'A Report to the Fund
for the Republic' (from which foundation he had ob-
tained a grant some years ago) the Fund did not
publish this strange work, it being meat too gamy
for even that charitable organization.

Mr. Kirk was wrong on three counts: (1) there was no circle of illiberal liberals on the C. U. campus, and the liberals who were there would not have considered me as the "most conspicuous"; (2) the Public Affairs Press in Washington was not a vanity press; and (3) I had never asked the Fund for the Republic to publish our report. Mrs. Harris and I assumed they would use it as a reference guide and that they would consider it as a kind of concluding report for the grant they had given us.

I asked Mr. Kirk and Mr. Buckley to withdraw their false statements but they refused to do so.

The Iowa Right Wing Collection has continued to grow and can now be purchased in microform.

The American Library Association 75th Anniversary Celebration and the American Heritage Program of Adult Education

As chairman of the A. L. A. 75th Anniversary Celebration Committee, I persuaded the committee to go along with the theme of trying to show how our heritage of political and social ideas as developed by the Founding Fathers could be useful in understanding the basic problems our country faced in 1952. We wanted this to be in contrast to the usual chauvinistic practice of reverence toward the older ideas without attempting a realistic application of them to today's problems.

To finance our plans Mr. Gardner Cowles, publisher of Look magazine and several Midwest newspapers, gave us $15,000. Our plans included the following: (1) We had Gerald Johnson write a book, This American People, in which he restated the essence of the early American ideas. (2) We had Henry Steele Commager edit an accompanying source book called Living Ideas in America, which we intended as a guide and source book for study groups A. L. A. was to organize throughout the country. Lay groups were contacted and the General Federation of Women's Clubs agreed to urge its members to use these books as study guides for their year's programs. Harper's agreed to publish both books, and Look magazine carried a lead article on the A. L. A. celebration. (3) We invited a group of distinguished Americans to address the A. L. A. Annual Conference on various aspects of the theme. They included the following: Professor John Wilson of the University of Chicago; Professor Jacques Maritain from

Princeton; Dr. Margaret Mead from the American Museum;
Professor Walter Laves from Indiana University, and Senator
Flanders from Maine. Each of these people spoke at a general session. The lectures were first rate. (4) The officers
of A. L. A. were seeking funds from the newly organized Ford
Foundation to finance the training of librarians as discussion
leaders in the adult education discussions that would follow up
the theme of the Conference. President Skip Graham, Exec-
cutive Secretary John Cory and I asked the officers of the
Ford Foundation for an appointment to discuss a grant, but
they said they weren't sufficiently well organized to make such
a grant. But as I reported later in reviewing the work of
our committee:

> In the meanwhile, the New York Public Library's
> 'Exploring the American Idea' program, of a parallel
> nature, attracted the attention of Scott Fletcher of
> the Ford Foundation and he approached John Cory
> to see if ALA would accept a grant to enlarge the
> scope of that kind of program. Fortunately, Mr.
> Cory was able to describe the operation and intent
> of our Heritage program, and in June, 1951, in-
> formed Mr. Fletcher that the ALA Executive Board
> would 'be pleased to accept a possible grant, and
> would be ideally situated to announce an American
> Heritage community discussion project as the vital
> next step in the 75th Anniversary program being
> celebrated in Chicago July 8-14 with the theme,
> "The American Heritage in Time of Crisis." ("The
> ALA's Anniversary: an Appraisal.")'

The grant was announced at the Chicago Meeting and
Mrs. Grace Stevenson was appointed to set up the experiment-
al projects. Later, many public libraries throughout the
country did organize adult discussion groups around the theme
of the American Heritage in Time of Crisis, and both the
Johnson and Commager books were widely used. It is impossible, of course, to evaluate the effect of this program.

One interesting side effect: the right wing groups,
whose publications I was collecting at Iowa, were very suspicious of the A. L. A. program, probably because they thought
of Commager and Johnson as liberals, if not worse. In one
of their publications (I can no longer remember which one this
was, and I have no way of tracking it down) they wished they
could put their finger on the one person they felt was behind
all of these discussion groups, and they tried to find out from

David Clift. David refused to tell them what they wanted to know, and I was glad he did. Skip Graham, John Cory and I would have had some bad publicity.

How I Almost Played Poker with President Harry S Truman

For many years several of us friends in ARL gathered after the evening sessions for a game of poker. Bob Miller, Bill Dix, Ben (and now and then Betsy) Powell, Gene Wilson, Flint Purdy and Cecil Bird were the regulars. We played what we called WPA poker, which meant that one could stay in and draw hands (but not raise the betting) even after he had lost the limit of money we agreed upon in advance--usually $5.00. These games were relaxed and friendly and we never discussed library matters at them. I was probably the poorest poker player in the group.

During the winter before A. L. A. was to meet in Kansas City in June 1957, it occurred to me that it would be fun to ask former President Harry S Truman to play with us. So I wrote to him, explaining our WPA rules. My letter and his reply are as follows:

February 8, 1957

The Honorable Harry S. Truman
Independence,
Missouri

Dear Mr. Truman:

The following group of University Librarians do invite you to join us for an evening of poker in Kansas City sometime during the week of the American Library Association meetings there - June 23-29, 1957.

All of us admire you, and we are all good ripsnorting Democrats. As to our poker playing ability -- well, we don't brag. We know that we would enjoy playing with you, and we think you would like us.

To be sure, we play for low stakes (two bit limit, three

raises per round -- and a $5.00 limit, W. P. A. poker), but on principle, you can't object to that! If you clean us, which is possible, we wouldn't object if you used the money to buy a first edition of Hoyle for the Truman Library.

There would be no publicity on this from us. This is not a stunt -- we play regularly twice a year at our conventions. We like you, and we would enjoy playing poker with you.

As soon as you accept our invitation, we will let you know the time and the hotel room number -- unless, of course, you would prefer to select the time and place. Any night between June 23 and 27 would be all right with us.

Sincerely,

Ralph Ellsworth, Director of Libraries, State University of Iowa, Iowa City, Iowa

Eugene Wilson, Director of Libraries, University of Colorado

William Dix, Librarian, Princeton University

Robert Miller, Director of Libraries, Indiana University

Cecil Byrd, Associate Director of Libraries, Indiana University

Ben Powell, Director of Libraries, Duke Univ.

Please send your reply to Ralph E. Ellsworth, Director of Libraries, State University of Iowa, Iowa City, Iowa

(For President Truman's reply see page 82.)

So, when we got to Kansas City June 24th I called his office, as instructed, to make the arrangements. Rose Conway, his secretary, told me that Mr. Truman would be unable to play with us because Margaret had just given birth to her first child, and the Trumans had left for New York the day before. She said Mr. Truman was extremely sorry he couldn't play with us.

HARRY S. TRUMAN
FEDERAL RESERVE BANK BUILDING
KANSAS CITY 6, MISSOURI

March 7, 1957

Dear Mr. Ellsworth:

I more than appreciated your kind letter of February
8th signed by you and your colleagues. It arrived while I
was in Florida, and I did not see it until my return to the
office the day before yesterday.

Your suggestion has a great amount of merit, and I
feel certain I could afford to make a contribution. When
you came to this suburb of Independence, please telephone
me, and we'll see if it isn't possible for us to get together.
It seems that you and I speak the same language.

Sincerely yours,

Harry Truman

Mr. Ralph E. Ellsworth
Director of Libraries
State University of Iowa
Iowa City, Iowa

So, that's how I almost got to play poker with President Truman. It's fun to speculate on what would have happened had we played and had he lost his $5.00. Which one of us would get his $5.00 bill? Or supposing, which was likely, he had beat all of us and then what would he have done with the $30.00? And who, afterwards, would have kept the deck of cards we played with? All kinds of problems might have arisen to create dissension among six old friends. Perhaps it's just as well the game was cancelled. Still ... ?

Speaking of poker, two other incidents are worth mentioning.

At the 1947 A. L. A. Conference in San Francisco, our poker group, which had been on some kind of tour, was trying, with no success, to hail a taxi to the St. Francis Hotel, where we were to have our game. John Burchard, Director of Libraries at MIT, and I were at the curb when along came an empty bus. We hailed it and asked the driver if we could hire him to take us to the St. Francis. He said we couldn't but to jump in and he would dump us off on his way to the barn. So our small group rode in regal splendor from the auditorium to the St. Francis, where, to the amazement of the crowds, we disembarked. We tipped the driver $2.00.

Another time at a Minneapolis A. L. A. Conference, my wife and I were staying with friends in a suburb. The ARL poker group was to play poker at Dean McDiarmid's house. After an enjoyable evening of poker, during which Cecil Bird won enough money to buy a Harris Tweed jacket (or so we have claimed), one of the group dropped me off at our friend's house. At 3 a. m. I woke up with a start, remembering that I had driven our car to the poker party and that it was still there. Pulling trousers over my p. j. s, I called a taxi, drove to the McDiarmid's and retrieved our car. In the morning, I was reminded by several members of my family that I had not only lost my poker money but had also run up an expensive taxi bill. I blamed it all on Hamm's beer.

Although the more-or-less-same group played poker for many years, wins and losses were pretty evenly divided, except when Betsy Powell (Mrs. Benjamin Powell) played with us. She invariably was the big winner. She was the only female allowed to invade our male sanctuary--male chauvinism not being illegal at that time!

I RETURN TO COLORADO

It is usually difficult to explain to flatlanders just why living
in Boulder, Colorado is so satisfactory. The beauty of the
mountains, the mild climate, the low humidity, the quick access to trout streams, all are parts of the reason. When
you get up in the morning you don't have to wring the water
out of your socks before putting them on in the summer, nor
do you in the winter time have to drive your car down sets
of ice tracks--like streetcar rails--the way we had to do in
Iowa City much of the time. When you wake up in the morning you first look at the sun on the mountains and then you
feel like charging down to the office to lick the hell out of
problems you might have left there, unsolved, the previous
day. To be sure, salaries are lower, there are more nuts
per city block than in the Midwest, the universities don't enjoy as high a status as do the big Midwest universities, and
the cost of living is higher, partly because of the cost of
shipping things over the mountains (even though Boulder is
on the east side). Also, the State Legislature, which in recent years has been dominated by red-neck Republicans, can
do some irrational things to the University--for example,
their attempt in 1978-79 to downgrade research in the University.

My fourteen years at the University of Iowa were good
years for many reasons. The quality of the faculty, and especially their wives, was very high. The long, cold, and se-
vere winters, plus the lack of diverting recreational facilities
in the area, plus the University traditions, made it easy for
the faculty to keep out of trouble by working very hard. One
could get a lot of work done there.

The Iowa years were therefore good from a professional point of view. Also, the University did allow me to
spend my summers at our mountain cabin in Colorado (a fact
the other deans grumbled about). But the family and I pined
for the mountains during the winters and longed for the sun-
shine and to see the deer and the antelope play! Also, it
seemed to me that the University of Iowa had reached a plateau

of excellence in many of its programs, whereas the University of Colorado, under the leadership of President Quigg Newton, was about to shed its old skin and to become a university of high quality. The chance to participate in this exciting effort had great appeal to me.

And so when E. H. Wilson moved out from his library post to the Deanship of Faculties (I insist there is no administrative post in a university that is up from the directorship of the libraries), I was asked if I would like to return to Colorado. I was then fifty years old--the age, I had heard, at which men often run off with other men's wives, or take to heavy drinking and other bad habits--and ready to try slaying a new herd of dragons. I was glad to come back to Colorado. My friends reminded me that moving from a larger, more prestigious university to a smaller one with less prestige might result in my going to pot, and to other forms of decay. I ignored these warnings and am very glad I did, because my years at Colorado since 1958 have continued to be stimulating, exciting and productive in every way.

Prior to World War II, the University of Colorado had been an excellent teaching university with very few Ph. D. -level programs. It took the position that it was better to turn out strong holders of M. A. degrees, who would then go to other universities for their doctorates. But following World War II many young people who had been in Boulder, and elsewhere in Colorado, for war effort programs flocked back determined to find ways of making a living there. The University of Colorado expanded its programs extensively until today it has some 50 Ph. D.-level programs and its enrollment has expanded five-fold.

But somehow, during this period of rapid expansion the library got left behind, perhaps because administrative leaders who are good at leading universities into rapid expansion are frequently not the kind of educatiors who see the need for strong libraries. At any rate, my assignment from President Newton was to bring the level of library service up to the level of the rest of the University. Had he known at the time how much money would be needed to do that, I think he would not have welcomed me so heartily.

Those were heady years for me, especially during the time Oswald Tippe was our provost. The newer research-minded faculty were ready for an improved library service. I got off to a good start with the faculty by keeping them informed of my intentions through a series of informal letters. In one of these I tried to pave the way for our intention to adopt the L. C. classification system and fuller use of L. C. catalog cards by saying that newly acquired books would go through the cataloging department like corn through a duck. Another time I explained that the library, far from being the heart of the University, could better be described in anatom- ical terms as being an organ located somewhere between the coccyx and the navel. Such corny and undignified tactics guaranteed readership of my letters, which was what I was after. Somewhat later an administrative decision forbade sending letters to the faculty; any such were now to be printed in an official University newspaper. I lost my magic.

Thanks to wise choices of associate directors--Joe Howard, now at the Library of Congress; Carl Jackson, now at Indiana; Richard Dougherty, now at Michigan; and Leo Cabell, still at Colorado--and a lively and able corps of li- brarians, the library was able to expand rapidly in terms of budgets, collections, space, and staff.

Much of my time during the first years was spent planning the reorganization of the library, getting ready for a library addition, fighting for a larger budget, and such. After having worked in a modular library at Iowa I became painfully aware of what it meant to try to meet new condi- tions and growth in a fixed-function building. The subject divisional plan was abandoned; the books were reshelved in classification order and, under Carl Jackson's leadership, the mechanization of the library's operations began, to be con- tinued under Richard Dougherty. Long-range plans for the library were prepared, and funds for a library addition were sought. To house the rapidly growing book collection, while waiting for the addition, we were forced to create several departmental libraries, not as a matter of policy, but of necessity.

Following is a brief account of some of the projects I was involved with until my retirement in 1972.

Conducting Seminars on Building Planning

In August 1964, the Educational Facilities Laboratories, Inc. asked me to organize a seminar in Boulder to help train twen- ty or so librarians to become knowledgeable consultants on

planning academic library buildings. Keyes Metcalf, William
Jesse and I shared responsibility for the lectures, which
lasted five days. EFL selected the librarians and also invited several architectural firms to attend. Most of the par-
ticipants felt that the sessions were worthwhile, but in a survey the University made of those who had attended, one librarian from the South said he hadn't learned a single thing!
Keyes, Bill and I couldn't decide whether this was our fault
or his.

In 1966, the York University School of Applied Architecture in York, England, asked Keyes and me to conduct a
similar seminar for British librarians and architects. There
were three long sessions each day for five days, and we
worked very hard. Keyes was in very bad health at the time,
and we were scared stiff he wouldn't live through each session. But like the proverbial firehorse, once each session
started he was strong as ever. Mrs. Metcalf waited outside
the session rooms, considerably worried. A few weeks later
Keyes had open heart surgery, but not until after he had gone
on to Ireland for some consulting work following the York
seminars. Luckily, he's been going strong ever since, and
it is generally believed that if there is such a thing as an
immortal man, Keyes is it.

We held our York meetings in a medieval church that
had been remodeled by the Institute. The sessions were
taped, and H. Faulkner Brown, an excellent architect, took on
the task of editing the tapes and publishing them in book form
--which Keyes and I both opposed. Faulkner's wife told me
later that she was so sick of my voice coming out of his study
that had she been able to lay hands on me she would have
choked me to death. Keyes and I felt that since our lectures
were prepared for informal, oral delivery, they would not
read well, especially after a five-year delay.

While the lectures were in session Theda explored the
city of York, including walking the wall, a unique experience.
She also kept track of the restoration work going on at the
Minster. Both Keyes and I were so tired at the end of each
day that we ate our dinners and went to bed. But not those
indefatigable Britishers. They sat up to all hours drinking
beer and arguing--probably the best part of the seminars for
them.

To prepare myself for these lectures I spent the month
of May with Theda, visiting the new Robbins (Provincial) Uni-

versity Libraries. (I had seen most of the Red Bricks as
well as Oxford and Cambridge on a previous trip.) Naturally,
we saw as many of the beautiful parts of England, Scotland,
and Wales as we could. We drove some 3,000 miles in a
rented car, mostly on the "wrong" side of the road, with
little difficulty. The roundabouts, however, sometimes presented problems; we found it hard to be sure which exit to
take. The result was that we usually had to go around several times, and then because of the lack of route signs, had
to drive several miles before we were sure we were on the
right road. I didn't put a scratch on the rented car until
near the end of the trip, when some blasted American ran
into the rear corner of the car while it was parked in a hotel parking lot. It turned out that we were both renting from
the same agency, so there was no problem settling the claim.
Nevertheless my pride was hurt.

We ended our touring with a week in the Lake District,
a few miles below Keswick in the Marymount Hotel, where I
wrote my lectures. In between rain showers we would dash
out, jump in the car and drive over a new pass or out into
the countryside to enjoy that most beautiful part of the world.
Ms. Mosely, the proprietress, made us special sandwiches
for lunch, with a pint of bitter for me and a pot of tea for
Theda. I also went fishing one day in the Derwent Water and
caught an eight-inch trout.

We ended our trip with a several-day visit with the
MacKenna at Glasgow, where we were taken on daily excur-
sions into the Trussacks and other beautiful places near Glasgow. It was here that we learned of the Volcano, a marvelous device for heating water for tea out in the wilds. We
now own three of these, one for ourselves and one for each
son. Mr. MacKenna joined us on a train ride from Glasgow
to York, where the sessions were being held.

The School Library Book

One day in 1961 as I sat napping in my office in Boulder, a
rather shy young man introduced himself as Jonathan King, a
staff member from Educational Facilities Laboratory, Inc.,
about which I knew nothing. He said he had come to persuade
me to do a book on school library space planning. I protested
that I knew little about school libraries having specialized in
college and university libraries. He replied that he had read

some of my stuff and that he was sure my iconoclastic approach was just what they wanted to break through the deadly
boredom of existing school libraries. (He obviously knew
how to reach my Achilles heel.) That line nearly got me but
when he showed me a letter written by the Executive Secretary of the A. L. A. School Libraries Division urging Educational Facilities Laboratory not to have me do the book, on
the grounds that I wasn't a school librarian and consequently
couldn't know anything about them, that did it. I agreed at
once to write the book. It was to be a collaboration between
an architect and me. They had chosen Professor Colbert,
then Dean of the Columbia University School of Architecture.

To prepare myself I read the literature, which seemed
to be barren and unimaginative, and I visited a few school
libraries. Only one, the University of Chicago Laboratories
School Library, came anywhere near living up to the potential
I had in mind. Next I read what the educators had to say
and I found out that they had nearly nothing to say about school
libraries, and totally nothing about their physical setting.
There were no school libraries in public schools that had as
many as 20,000 books.

Next I went into seclusion at our mountain cabin and
wrote out what I called a "matrix" statement--a pouring out
of whatever was in my head on the subject of school libraries.
This was wild and woolly, but out of it I could see a sensible
book emerging. Soon after that Dean Colbert joined me for
a long weekend discussion at our cabin. If my "matrix"
thoughts were in the clouds, his were in the stratosphere.
I didn't know what he was talking about and had the distinct
impression he didn't either. The feeling was probably mu-
tual. Ruth Weinstock, the Educational Facilities Laboratory
editor assigned to the project, tried to make some sense out
of our efforts, but concluded it was hopeless. Dean Colbert
withdrew from the project and Educational Facilities Laboratory employed Hobart Wagener, a Boulder architect, to do
the graphics--which he did with fine results. I'm sure it was
his drawings rather than my text that made the book such a
success, but much credit should also be given to the photographs selected by Ruth Weinstock, many of which speak with
greater effect than do the words of the text. Ruth Weinstock
wrestled with my text--every sentence of it--and cleaned it
up considerably, catching me up on my prejudices against
school administrators and infusing some ideas of her own.

Educational Facilities Laboratory has distributed over

90, 000 copies of this book. EFL and I received dozens of letters from school administrators, school planners and school librarians, all favorable. The ones from school administrators interested me especially, because they disproved my prejudices against them. They said the ideas in the book were just what they had been looking for, but had been unable to get out of the school library group. I shall not resist the temptation of saying that I have never heard one word from the school library establishment within A. L. A. , or from any professor teaching school library courses in an American library school.

The appearance of this book apparently coincided with the appearance of the concept of open planning in elementary and secondary schools and one can now see hundreds of highly imaginative and heavily used school library areas in these schools all over the country.

I have neglected to say that on one of my trips to England, the year before I wrote the book, I had seen in the Ifield Lower School, south of London, a highly imaginative, living model of what I thought a school library should be like. And now may I pay tribute to the Headmaster, Mr. Arthur Worthy, who on a Saturday morning brought several of the teachers and students back to school to demonstrate for us how an "infused" school library could work. As a reward for the work the students had done, they were allowed an extra swim that morning in the school pool.

And after the demonstration Mr. Worthy took us and Mr. Roy Fenton, our host, to the Plough, a very, very old pub, for sherry. One of the best days in England.

VISITING AND CONSULTING WITH FOREIGN LIBRARIES

In 1958, as part of the preparation for the book I was doing
for Ralph Shaw's State of the Library Art series, I went to
Great Britain and Europe to study new library buildings.   I
visited some of the red brick universities in England as well
as in Edinburgh and Glasgow, one or two in France, one in
Sweden and several in Germany.   Anthony Thompson, who
was at the time Secretary of IFLA, drove me to Cambridge
to see the addition to their central library immediately after
a sleepless twelve-hour flight in a DC-6 from Detroit to London.

     While we waited in the foyer of the Cambridge Library
to be announced, we watched the factotum, or porter, bawl
hell out of a young undergraduate who tried to enter the library without his black gown.   He didn't get in.   The Cambridge addition seemed cold and unhuman to me, but the thing
that impressed me most was the series of "closed" catalogs,
each representing a time period in the library's history.

     At a later date, 1972, I watched while a man proudly
pasted small slips into the library's book catalog.   In reply
to my question as to what he would do when a page became
filled up, he said he would remove the slips with his knife
and rearrange them properly on new pages, which could be
inserted into the catalog.   The Head Librarian on that visit
told me that in spite of considerable sentiment in favor of
keeping the old book catalog, he was determined to modernize
the process but wasn't sure which way to go--to microform,
as at Birmingham University, or to wait until a computerized
system was ready.

     One of the really horrible experiences of my life oc-
curred that evening.   I had managed to get an hour's sleep
in Thompson's Bedford Van between Cambridge and London,
and after a nice cup of tea I attempted to make a speech before a group of London librarians interested in buildings--at
6 p. m. I spoke in a church, I think, from an elevated lectern,
which made me dizzy and uncomfortable.   To this day I have

no idea of what I told them, but I'm sure it must have been awful. They didn't throw tomatoes at me, but I thought they might. Had I known about jet lag then, I think I might have persuaded Anthony to postpone the lectures.

In 1964 I attended the SCONUL (Standing Committee on National and University Libraries) sessions at Hull University as part of the ARL delegation from the United States and between sessions I was able to study the new Hull Library and also the British Lending Library at Boston Spa. The latter we found to be a remarkably efficient system designed by an imaginative physicist-librarian, Donald Urquhart. We, the Vospers and Marion Milczewski, our traveling companions, were invited after the SCONUL conference to the Urquharts for dinner.

Mr. Urquhart defended the lack of a catalog of the library's holding on the grounds that if one went to the shelves and the book you wanted wasn't there, in its proper alphabetical order, or if it weren't charged out, then the library didn't own it--certainly a money-saving idea even if it was somewhat faulty in logic. His system of an overhead carrier for correspondence and books on route to the mail or copying room was an interesting combination of the money-carriers department stores formerly used for getting money from the clerk to the cashier who sat in a kind of bird's nest on an upper mezzanine level, and the Louden manure-carriers farmers used to transport the stuff from the animals' stall to the manure pile some distance from the barn. Mr. Urquhart said he had seen both systems. In the new library, all systems are highly mechanized and computerized. Mr. Urquhart, the late Angus S. Macdonald and Dr. Douglas Waples are, in my opinion, the three most imaginative men in the modern library scene. The late Ralph Shaw probably should be included with them.

It was on the sightseeing trip after SCONUL that we, the Vospers and Marion, stayed at the Rose and Crown Hotel in Wisbach, which had five bars, one of which, the Cellar, served seven kinds of sherry. At the Cellar bar we had a lovely conversation with the barmaid, who claimed she could jump over the bar to serve the customers (there seemed to be no other way), and who proved it by jumping over it for us. I took her picture just after the leap.

As well as visiting many foreign libraries, it has been my privilege to serve as a consultant on several.

Sweden. Stockholm University

In the winter of 1973 Jan Seth, an architect with the Swedish Board of Public Buildings, visited United States libraries in anticipation of a new library for Stockholm University.   In addition to going on a skiing expedition with Leo Cabell, Mr. Seth discussed problems of library planning with me.   Later, I was invited to serve as Stockholm's consultant.

Planning libraries in Sweden is different in many ways from planning in the United States.   In the first place, all educational and cultural institutions and their buildings are owned by the government.   They are under the control of the National Board of Public Buildings, which has its own staff of architects (Jan Seth for the Stockholm project) and which oversees each project closely.   In addition to this board, the city of Stockholm has a Commission on Libraries, and then of course there are the administration and faculty committees. The students of the university have their own union, with real power.   The president of the student union and its legal ad-viser attended each session of every committee and they voted as full partners.   Jan Seth proved to be an intelligent, pro-gressive and scholarly architect, with the ability to carry a project through the maze of boards, etc., to completion.   His death, just as the project was ready to be presented to the National Board, came close to spelling doom to the project on a crucial issue--site, as I shall explain.

When I arrived on the scene in May 1974 there were two possible sites.   One would combine the existing science library on the north side of the mall and the humanities and social science library on the south side in one building in the center of the mall, but not connected to either academic build-ing.   The other site would place the library west of the mall but separated from it by a wooded hill.   This site had the advantage of being close to the bus station and to the Student Union building.   Stockholm's weather, with its cold, dark winters, made the issue of site an important one.

I should explain that the Frescati campus, located on the edge of Stockholm, housed the humanities and social sci-ences in a massive six-level structure with a series of wings on the side opposite the mall.   The library was housed in one level of a two-story structure running the length of the human-ities building, some 600 feet long and about sixty feet wide. Obviously the shape of the library made it impossible to manage efficiently.

Five architectural firms had been selected to participate in an architectural competition. Each firm was invited
to make use of my services during the two weeks I was
there. Only one firm--run by Ralph Erskine, an English
architect who had lived in Stockholm for many years--seemed
to know how to make use of a consultant, and he did just that.
It was his firm that won the competition!

Two things seemed quite obvious to me: first, the
science faculties wouldn't tolerate moving their library to a
building not connected to theirs; and second, in view of the
climate and design of the social science and humanities building the new library should be connected so that the faculties
and students could go from their offices to the library without going outdoors. I urged each firm to take these two
points seriously. Only one did.

To make a long and complex story short (being a half-
Swede I know how Swedes love to take a long time to chew
things over), the student union, the librarians, and the faculty committees endorsed my two points. I appeared before
the National Board to urge them to accept both points, but
there was opposition on both issues. Jan Seth died at this
stage in the negotiations. Ralph Erskine's drawings seemed
best to me, and to the faculty committees, the librarians and
the student union. He was finally selected by the National
Board to do a building within the mall that would adjoin the
social science and humanities structure. The sciences were
to keep their own library.

To celebrate the victory, the night before I left for
home the Rector gave a dinner for those involved and for what
I suppose was the power structure within the university. After
the usual cocktails, graceful toasts, short speeches and an
excellent dinner, the party broke up. At this point the Rector said, rubbing his hands in expectation, "Now the real
drinking begins." At this point I left to pack my bags and
get some sleep in anticipation of an early morning flight
home. En route to the airport the next morning, Thomas
Tottie, my host, and I got so engrossed talking that he drove
by the airport turnoff and we nearly missed my flight.

I made two trips to Sweden for this project, which is
now under construction after considerable delay caused by a
government ban on air conditioning for public buildings. The
Erskine plans are beautiful and highly functional and I am certain the library will be a great success, one of the best in
northern Europe.

Iran. The Pahlavi Imperial Library and Center

Dr. Herman Liebaers, then Librarian of the Belgian Royal
Library in Brussels, invited me to join a team of four librarians and architects (Malcolm Wilson from the British
Museum expansion projects, M. Segun from the French Bib-
liotèque Nationale addition, Herr Leabers from a German
University and myself) to go to Teheran in August 1973 to
advise the government on how to go about planning a new Imperial Library and Cultural Center. The government was to
pay our travel costs but there were to be no consultation
fees.

Since I had never had an opportunity to see the clas-
sical sights of Greece I decided to make a stopover in Athens
to rest en route and to visit a few places--which I did for a
few days. I was scheduled to fly from Athens to Teheran on
a Sunday afternoon, and, after checking in, I was waiting for
our KLM flight departure when the terrorists broke into the
lower waiting room and began throwing grenades and shooting
people with machine guns. The noise was paralyzing but
somehow I managed to get up the stairway and out of the
building without getting hit. Others were killed and many
were wounded.

There were at the time some 5,000 people in the airport building, many on the upper observation level watching
the planes come and go. Those people were not allowed to
leave the building until later, but some did get out. We
gathered on the lawn outside while ambulances drew up to
carry out the wounded on stretchers, and the dead in sacks.
Soldiers and high officials in limousines dashed up. Standing
next to me was a young Greek couple tearfully awaiting news
of the relatives they had taken to the airport for departure
on the El Al plane whose passengers were the object of the
terrorists' attack. I asked them if when they got home they
would be willing to send a cable to my wife saying that I was
safe. They agreed gladly and I left money with them to cover
the cost. They did send the cable, and my wife got it, just
minutes before she saw the TV news of the bombing.

After two hours of standing around, not knowing what
to do, we heard a KLM official with a bull horn rounding up
the people scheduled to go out on my flight. We were taken
to the KLM downtown office and after considerable delay were
paired off and sent to a hotel. My partner turned out to be
a young German salesman who knew no English or Greek and

who had never been in Athens before. My German was good
enough so that we could communicate. After we checked in
I sent another cable to my wife (which she never got), and
one to my host in Teheran (which he never got).

At dinner we were not exactly cheered when the maître
d' told us that the restaurant had been shot up the previous
week.

During the evening KLM told us we would be flying
out Monday night on SAS. That gave us all day Monday to
see the sights again and another chance to spend time at the
Acropolis.

Our SAS plane left on schedule and we arrived in Teheran about 2 a. m. Standing near the entrance door was a
young man with a sign with my name on it. It seemed that
my host, Dr. Shafa, had not received my cable, and, not
knowing when I would arrive or what had happened to me,
had stationed a young man at the airport to meet all incoming
planes from Athens. He whisked me around customs and
drove me directly to the Inter-Continental Hotel where a room
was waiting for me. My suitcase arrived the next day. I
tried to sleep but was still shaking from the bombing episode
--the most horrifying experience in my life.

Next morning I met Mr. Liebaers and some of the
others in the dining room and was informed that at 10:00 I
was to make my report. I had no report prepared. I had
not expected to be called upon to do this, and I had considerable difficulty in organizing a presentation. It wasn't that
I didn't know what to say, but that my brain still didn't function properly.

Our host, Dr. S. Shafa, Deputy Minister for Cultural
Affairs to the Imperial Court and Director of the Pahlavi Library, was in charge of the project, which was to be not only
an Imperial Library but also a National Cultural Center with
facilities for scholarly conventions, a Center for Islamic
Studies, a Public Library for Teheran, etc.

The first day we were taken for a session with the
Teheran City Planning Commission, which consisted of some
three thousand young people busy planning for a city of twelve
million people. This division was headed by a very intelligent M. I. T. graduate and I was favorably impressed with
what I saw of the staff's work. The enthusiasm was conta-
gious and we were excited by the prospects ahead.

Our usual daily schedule was as follows: from 9 a. m.
until 1:30 p. m. we worked as a committee on various aspects
of our project. At 1:30 Dr. Shafa would take us to an elegant
restaurant for a long leisurely lunch. We then went back to
the hotel for a swim or a nap until late in the afternoon, when
we were taken to see some of the sights of the city. At 8
p. m. we were picked up at the hotel and taken to another
restaurant, where we usually dined until around 1:30 a. m.

Dr. Shafa's large black Lincoln limousine was, so we
were told, the only one in Teheran, and everyone seemed to
recognize him and his tall, dignified driver. In fact, when
we came to a red light, if there was a policeman on duty he
would stop the traffic and wave us through. Our driver drove
very fast but, to our amazement, traffic parted ahead of us
as though we were the Israelites walking through the Red Sea.
It was fun but a little scary and embarrassing too. Since the
only people in Teheran with beards (except me) were the
whirling dervishes, the natives seemed startled to see one
tall, white bearded man, with two plump German and Belgian
librarians on either side of him in the back seat of the Lincoln. Dr. Shafa rode in the front seat with the driver.

There weren't, apparently, many tourist sights to see
in Teheran. We went to a new, highly sculptured Museum,
where we saw a brilliantly assembled visual story of the accomplishments of Iran under the Shah. At my request we
were taken to a large Mosque--a beautiful building. Inside
there were small tables where men could sit, talk and drink
coffee. But this area was divided from the back part of the
Mosque, where the women could sit--but with no table, and
presumably no coffee. Across the courtyard within the Mosque
complex there were several young men living, studying for
the priesthood.

On our tour we were driven past several Imperial libraries, one of which was under construction. I gathered
that these were to be absorbed into the new Imperial Library.

We were driven through the slums, which indeed did
smell bad, and past the maternity hospital, built by the Empress. We were told that she went there to have her children, which endeared her to the poor people of the city. We
were also told that the Empress had built a heart research
center and hospital, the best in the Middle East, but we did
not see it. We also saw one of the older palaces where distinguished visitors were put up (President and Mrs. Nixon had

just been there). We thought the InterContinental Hotel was
a better place for us. We did not see the Shah or his family.

During the time I was in Iran I had no Iranian money,
nor any use for any. Every cent of my expenses was paid
by our host--even the newspaper we read. I did no shopping.
At the end of our five days of work, the rest of our party
went south to Isfahan and Shiraz, but I was still so upset by
the Athens bombing that I flew home as quickly as possible.

Claudine Desmets, a young French girl, a member of
Dr. Shafa's staff at the Pahlavi Library, handled all our local
arrangements. She accompanied me to the airport (in the
Lincoln), and as I boarded the plane she handed me two cans
of caviar with instructions to keep them on ice--which was
no problem on the airplane. But when I got to Chicago about
midnight I discovered that my flight from Chicago to Denver
had been cancelled and I was put up at the airport hotel at
O'Hare. I decided that I wasn't going to trust my caviar to
the hotel staff, so I improvised a refrigerator out of an over-
turned plastic wastebasket, a wet towel and ice cubes. It
worked fine and my caviar arrived in Denver in fine condition.

The Iranian team we worked with on the library project included two beautiful young women, one a computer expert and the other an architect, and a team of men--archi-
tects and planners. These were the only Iranians we talked
with while we were there. These women, and many others
we met two years later at a meeting on Long Island, were
completely Westernized in terms of self-esteem, education,
attitudes, professional competence and dress. As I watch
the women protestors today on TV (March 1979) I expect to
see their faces. I cannot believe that these women, and thousands like them, will willingly accept Khomeini edicts.

Our last day's duties consisted of each of us writing
a report on his share of the discussion topics. The project
at that time had a 40-million-dollar price tag. Two years
later, under Nasser Sharify's direction, the budget was up
some 225 million dollars. A team of some forty consultants
and others have, under Sharify's direction, produced an eight-
volume Program, and, as I understand it, an architectural
competition has been held. What the fate of the project will
be, or what has happened to Dr. Shafa, I do not know.

Saudi Arabia.   Riyadh University

Dr. Robarts of the Ford Foundation asked me to go to Riyadh
in April 1974 to review plans the University had prepared for
enlarging the present temporary library building on its downtown campus.   I was joined there by Atallah Doany, a Jor-
danian architect, who, as it happened, had visited me earlier
in Boulder.

After a very long flight from Denver I arrived at the
Dahran airport at 5 a. m. only to watch the customs man pour
my quart of whiskey into a barrel--somehow I hadn't known
it was forbidden in Saudi Arabia.   I was met at Riyadh a
couple of hours later by two librarians--Dr. Al Mani and Mr.
Hug--and was checked into a rather austere hotel.   But shortly I was taken from there to the Ford Foundation guest house,
where we stayed.   This modest house, with three bedrooms
and a room in the rear for the cook, was located on an un-
named and unpaved street, with the inevitable wall around the
yard.   Goats roamed the streets, fed, it was said, by the
garbage tossed over the walls.   Our cook, a young Yemenese,
did his best, but the menu consisted of a chopped tomato and
lettuce salad and either frozen chicken or steak, with ice
cream for dessert.   Corn flakes and scrambled eggs for
breakfast, and Pepsis (not Cokes) in the frig.   A driver for
the Ford Foundation took us to work each morning and picked
us up about 1:30 for lunch.   We had all afternoons and evenings for rest and discussion.   There was one restaurant in
town but we went there no more than once.   The food was
not very good.

Atallah and I agreed quickly that the plans that had
been drawn were entirely unsuitable, and we showed the Vice
Rector and architects how they should be redrawn.   We were
unfavorably impressed by the Egyptian architects and suggested
that the University could do better.   For example: since women students could not use the same reading rooms and other
library facilities as the men, the architects had proposed a
separate but adjacent reading room for the women, with the
card catalog located on a rotating platform between the two
reading rooms.   We wondered what would happen if there
happened to be a woman using the catalog when a man spun
it around, or vice versa.

I ended up by suggesting that they put their catalog records in machine-readable form, with terminals located in the
women's reading room and in the other branch libraries that

were located in several abandoned palaces around the city.
They already had a computer center in the university and the
engineering librarian was about to put his catalog in machine-
readable form.   I'm sure that by now they have done a thorough job of mechanizing their operations.   Some of the library
staff had already studied in American library schools, and the
rest were scheduled to do so in the near future.

I saw many strange anomalies on the campus, such
as faculty members lecturing slowly enough for students to
copy down every word--which one could see them memorizing
later.   On the other hand, they possessed the most sophisticated electronic teaching equipment then in existence.   Since
male faculty members could not lecture in the same room
with women students, a man would be lecturing into a TV
camera, while the women, in the next room, were listening
to the lecture on a TV screen.

I talked with a young Western-trained art teacher trying to teach future teachers in elementary schools how to in-
troduce art forms of a geometric nature, since the use of the
human figure in art is forbidden.

In each of the scientific departmental libraries the
books in English were on one side of the room and the books
in Arabic on the other side.   All teaching in science was done
in English, and most of the scientific faculty seemed to have
been trained in the United States.   The Vice Rector, I believe,
had his doctorate in History from Oxford.   Islamic studies
were, of course, taught in Arabic.

Dr. Wahaibi, a professor of Islamic studies, known
for his liberalism and sense of humor, had visited me pre-
viously in Boulder.   While in Riyadh I visited him in his home
four or five times, but I never met his wife, although she
obviously was present in the house.   Each day from 6 to 8
p. m. Dr. Wahaibi held open house in his parlor, and as many
as twenty to twenty-five men would drop by and sit quietly in
big overstuffed chairs placed around the edges of the room--
shoes left outside, of course.   Wahaibi's son served coffee
with great skill.   I say skill because it took skill to pour coffee into the small cups from those long spouted pots.   The
object seemed to be to pour with the cup a foot or two from
the pot.   I never learned how.

Some of the men came just to sit.   Others had questions of one kind or another.   One had a contract he wanted

Dr. Wahaibi to read before he signed it. Some visited with
their friends. Some were in Western business suits, but
most wore the Saudi native dress. Some were governmental
officials; some were business men. One man must have
been a laborer--he was barefooted and much weather-beaten,
as though he worked outdoors. Several came and sat next to
me and visited in a most friendly way. It was all quite relaxed. At 8 p.m. everyone disappeared.

The call to prayer five times a day, twenty minutes
each time, beginning at dawn, was broadcast by loud speakers
placed in the minarets all over town. I found it delightful to
be awakened each morning by the plaintive but penetrating
call. During the prayer times the TV stopped broadcasting
and during the day the stores were required to close. The
clerks all gathered on the sidewalks outside their stores. The
Wahaibi clergy were there with whips to see that the stores
were closed. I saw the block where convicted murderers
were beheaded.

Wesley Edwards, the Ford Foundation representative
in Riyadh, Atallah and I spent one evening wandering through
the downtown part of Riyadh. We noticed that someone had
left a sack of oranges on the trunk of his car, and later,
when we returned by the same route, the oranges were still
there even though the street was packed with passers-by. As
a test of what we had heard about the lack of crime, we
walked through a dark alley. It was pitch black, and although
we were aware that there were many people around us no one
bothered us; we felt perfectly safe.

The University officials threw a desert party for us
while we were there. We were driven about five miles into
the desert--flatland covered with low shrubs, much like the
San Luis Valley in Colorado--where we found two large tents.
In the first one we were seated on Oriental rugs and were
served dates and tea; these, we were told, were, with goat's
milk, a complete diet for the nomads. We visited there for
an hour or so and then were led into the second tent where
we found two large brass bowls (about three feet in diameter)
full of rice with a barbecued sheep on top of each. We squat-
ted in a ring around each bowl, each of us with a plate in
front of him. You were supposed to reach in with your fin-
gers and make a small ball of rice to pop into your mouth,
and then tear off a piece of sheep. They gave me a spoon
because I couldn't ball the rice. The sheep and rice were
delicious. Dr. Al Nafi, the Vice-Rector, pulled out a kidney

for me, perhaps to test me. It happens that kidney is one of my favorite foods, so I passed the test. He tried to pull out the tongue for me but couldn't get it out. He didn't try an eye, which might have given me some trouble.

While we ate, the servants stood behind us fanning us with towels to keep off the flies, which were present in large numbers. These men, who obviously had been working there all day, were very friendly and even consented to let me take their pictures--which is not generally allowed in Saudi Arabia. They too were masters at the art of pouring coffee into a cup from a distance of a foot or two, from the long spouted pots. I brought one home with me but have been unable to use it as the natives did.

In making our final report to the Vice-Rector, I suggested that as soon as they had put their own catalog into machine-readable form, they might work toward an all-Saudi network, and then eventually an all-Arab network. At that time they obviously would not have considered including Israel, but one might expect this attitude to change, eventually. The anti-Israel feeling showed itself in many ways. Products of companies that had factories in Israel were not allowed: for example, Coca Cola and Ford cars.

Since there were no Western-style men's or women's clothes for sale, there were no multi-story department stores. Most of the retail stores sold Japanese cameras, tape recorders, etc. --not much from the United States.

The campus the University was using in 1975 was temporary and plans were underway for a new one outside Riyadh. The University had contractual relations with Indiana University, and the library planning since has been done by Carl Jackson and others from Indiana.

The native talent, ability, desire, and drive to achieve and to modernize were all present in great abundance, but not, apparently, at the expense of rejecting the Moslem relgion. Now that Saudi Arabia has the money to finance the training of its people, it is moving quickly to the kind of library service the Saudis need and want. The willingness of their young librarians to spend two or three years of their lives abroad, often without their families, to get the education they need, left a deep impression on me. The people I worked with were superior in every way. One marvels at how all that talent could lie fallow for so many centuries and then suddenly blossom from the stimulus of an external influence.

In view of the lack of what we would consider recreational facilities I wondered what the Saudi people did for fun.
Obviously their work and religious practices kept them busy.
On Thursday afternoons the desert around Riyadh was filled
with camping families, some with tents and some without.
Each family had a fire and there was a circle of people cooking their food and eating, and of course visiting.   There was
a large race track outside Riyadh, but I never found out how
often it was used.   The annual camel race took place while
I was there, and the finish was broadcast on TV.   Plush chair
and carpets had been brought out for the Kind and friends
near the finish line.   The King seemed to enjoy the ceremony.

TV programs were broadcast daily after 6 p.m. , but
they seemed to consist mostly of Egyptian singers and news-
casts--interrupted by the prayer time.   We found little news
of the outside world.   Atallah spoke Arabic and he told me
what was going on.   Although I expected the customs and
mores in a strict Muslim state to be different, I was surprised by the censorship of foreign magazines practiced in
Saudi Arabia in 1974.   For example, the current issue of
Time received by the Ford Foundation guest house contained
an article about and a picture of Lady Godiva, nude, riding
her white horse in England.   This had been inked out, as
had several other paragraphs in the issue.   Advertisements
showing anatomy beyond the minimum were also inked out.

I was aware, of course, of the attitude of Muslims
toward the display of anatomy in art and in life, but I was
surprised that the government would bother to censor it in
imported magazines.   When I visualized the hundreds of men
busy each week and month with their felt-tipped pens going
through a new pile of magazines, after someone else had decided which items were verboten, I could see a large factory
of bored workers and a tremendous cost to the government.
And then I wondered if constant exposure to the forbidden and
immoral pictures wouldn't corrupt the censors.   Perhaps now,
since there are so many more foreigners, and thus more foreign magazines in the country, the practice has been discontinued.

Once a week the King held open house to anyone who
wanted to come and present a complaint or bring a message.
Members of the Royal Family occupied large and beautiful
palaces, each surrounded by the familiar wall.   I was told
that wealthy merchants also lived in similar homes.   In my
innocence I took a picture of one of the Prince's palaces, not

knowing that had I been detected by the police I would have been arrested. The police and military were, by the way, present everywhere in the central part of the city. I never saw them do anything but stand watching the people.

In addition to the Riyadh University project in Saudi Arabia, I also helped William Fellini, an Italian architect located in Rome, plan a library for an American military compound near Riyadh, but I have never seen the completed structure. This was all done by correspondence.

On my way home from Riyadh on the Iranian airline, after a refueling stop in Rome the steward came back onto the plane with a bottle of beer for each of us in the first class section of the plane. I noticed that there were several Saudi men in the first class section, while their wives and children were seated in the coach section.

I stayed overnight at a London airport hotel on my return. About midnight, just outside my room one of those two-tone European sirens let go with one hell of a blast. I think I hit the ceiling, and was sure we were in for another bombing episode. Our instructions were to run out into the street immediately if the siren went off, but remembering how hard it was raining, I didn't go. Room doors were opened cautiously and uncombed heads peered out. No one knew why the siren went off and the clerks at the desk refused to say. Maybe just a prank.

Venezuela. Simon Bolivar University

The Dean of the General College of Simon Bolivar University visited me in Boulder in 1974 to discuss the proposed library building project his University had in mind. I spent a week on the campus in January 1975 and helped write a building program for them. Unfortunately, Senora Teresa Martinez S., the librarian, was ill during the time I was there and couldn't participate in the discussions.

Simon Bolivar University is a new university located some twenty miles from the center of Caracas on an old private estate, of which the charming, rambling manor house has been retained as the administrative offices. Several of the classrooms, laboratories, studios and dormitories had been constructed, and the library was temporarily housed in a

building which was to be used for other functions when the
new library was completed.

There were several complicating factors in the planning process, in addition to the illness of the librarian.
First, there were no good nearby library buildings one could
use to illustrate the points I was trying to make. Second,
the kind and level of education and training possessed by the
library school graduates did not qualify them to serve ade-
quately in a university library. Third, the gentleman in
charge of campus planning, a friendly, generous and helpful
man whose experience had been in Germany, had compiled
all the relevant data in great detail. But his conception of
a university library was, quite naturally, based on the older
German library patterns, and as a result I had some difficulties in guiding the architect's work into plans that were
suitable for a Latin American university with modern intentions. And fourth, the Simon Bolivar University students had
one study habit that had to be respected but could not be allowed to dominate the reader-station layout of the library.
When they studied in the library they gathered around a table
and discussed, quite audibly, their study problems. I was
told that the habit was caused by the poor quality of the lower schools they had attended. The students were helping one
another with their study problems. But the result was that
the reading rooms were too noisy for anyone who wanted to
study alone in peace and quiet. The answer, of course, was
to build into the plans provisions for many group study rooms
and to distribute these rooms throughout the buildings so that
students would find them conveniently at hand. There were
to be, as a result, fewer individual tables and quite a few
individual study carrels.

The Rector of the University insisted that the library
be done right and that it provide seats for the same percentage of the enrollment that a high quality American university
provided, even though the budget did not provide enough money to do that. The architects submitted several editions of
the plans to me later in Boulder, and the last version seemed
satisfactory to me. I assume the building is now completed
and in use. I also suggested ways they could solve their
personnel problem.

Yugoslavia. Titograd University

Mrs. C. R. Zaher, then Director of the Division for the Development of Documentation, Libraries and Archives of Unesco, invited me to go to Titograd in the spring of 1975 to help with the planning of a library for the University. Unesco had been assisting the new university in several aspects of its formation: physical planning, language instruction, computer installation, and the library. My work was done under the direction of John Beynon, an American architect who was at that time in charge of school and college planning in various parts of the world, and with the advice of Kenneth Roberts, a staff member working with Mrs. Zaher. After a briefing in Paris, I spent two weeks in Titograd.

Titograd, the administrative and trade center of the Republic (State) of Montenegro in the Socialist Federal Republic of Yugoslavia, had been the center of the partisan forces under Tito in World War II. The Germans bombed the city flat and the armies tried without success to capture Citinje, the capital of Montenegro, which lies some twenty-five miles up in the mountains. Titograd is the center of a valley, with high and beautiful mountains on all sides, about thirty miles from the sea.

The University, a new institution, is made up of several pre-existing faculties and institutes in and around Titograd. There are three faculties at the university level--Economics, Engineering and Law--and three institutes--History (not included in the new University), Agriculture and Biological and Medical Research. Then, at Niksic, about thirty miles up in the mountains, there is a Pedagogical Acacemy, for the training of primary school teachers.

Each of these faculties and institutes retains its autonomy (and its library!)--but together they make up the new University, which has a new campus about three blocks from where the buildings for the three faculties are now located. There is one dormitory about to be finished on the new site, and the library is supposed to be next to be constructed.

The University is governed by an elected Council of fifty-one and an Executive Committee. It elects a Rector who serves for two years and can be reelected once. He is responsible to the Council.

The Institute of History, located across town, with its

library of some 30,000 books, had not agreed in 1975 to come into the University, although some of its professors taught a few courses in the University. This institute concerns itself almost entirely with Montenegran history.

Somehow, in this maze of decentralized units, most of the subjects one expects to find in an undergraduate university are to be found.

There is a nucleus of a central university library crowded into the halls of one of the Institute buildings. It owns about 5,000 mathematical books, all in Russian, and some 1,500 other books and unbound journals. The Russian books had been purchased, I was told, because they were cheap. All students study the Russian language, but whether they learn enough to use the language proficiently is doubtful. Each of the faculty libraries has a respectable but small reading room with a very small collection of books and journals. The central library has one librarian who has had some experience working in the Brussels Royal Library and in the Montenegran National Library in Citinje. She has had a university education. The Agricultural Institute owns about 8,000 books, Chemistry about 2,000, History 30,000 and Pedagogy some 75,000; but these do not belong to the University. In Citinje, the old capital of Montenegro, the national library owns some 800,000 books, mostly exchanges from the other republics. This library is housed in two old foreign embassies, the books in one and the staff in the other. The books are housed in terrible condition. There are very few users of this library, but if plans for a new building are carried out the library will be in usable shape, eventually. In 1975, to go from Titograd to Citinje one drove up a narrow, winding mountain road. It was easy to see why the Germans couldn't capture the city. A new road is promised (1975).

Nevertheless, even with a new building and a new road, it makes little sense for that library to be tucked away up in the hills, except that the people of the Republic attach much sentiment to the old capital, with its Royal Museum and historical memories. To move it to Titograd was not to be considered at the time I was there, and perhaps will never be.

The Pedagogical Library in Niksic is an important collection, but it, too, is housed in a series of over-crowded rooms and is inadequately staffed. There is an author catalog but no title or subject catalogs.

My recommendations included the obvious suggestion (which agreed with the intent of the Rector, who had studied at Florida State University) that as many as possible of the scattered collections be brought together in the new library building and that the University Librarian be given the authority to run the library in as unified a manner as possible. Their biggest problem is how to assemble a staff of librarians in time to acquire and make ready for use a collection of 200,000 books by the time the building is finished. I told them how this could be done if they could get enough hard currency to buy the service from abroad, and to send the head librarian abroad for some basic training in librarianship. There was talk of installing a computer connection with Zagreb, but it seemed to me they had to have a basic library first.

Mr. John Beynon and I worked out a set of basic plans, of a modular nature, that could be used to guide the architect who was to be employed. Some recent information on what has happened since suggests that he didn't follow our suggestions very closely.

During the first few days there I was taken to call on the heads of each of the Faculties and Institutes. Each of them, except the head of the History Institute, expected his collection to be merged. Each of these conferences, by the way, began with a glass of brandy and a cup of coffee. By the end of the day I felt pretty good.

Perhaps, since the country is so different from the United States or western Europe, a few comments of a non-library nature may be permitted.

One of the most delightful customs I witnessed was the evening "Paseo." Each evening at 6 p.m. everyone turned out to walk the length of the main street, which was then closed to auto traffic. Young and old, boys and girls, walked the length of the street, nearly a mile, up one side of the street and down the other. Here boy met girl, people visited and gossiped, strangers enjoyed looking at the people. The procession stopped at midnight, when presumably people went home to bed. A delightful pastime.

During the week I caught a frightful cold and cough and my host insited that I visit a doctor at their new hospital. The doctor was a young, intelligent, and well-informed man. He was assisted by a nurse who had worked in the Mayo Clinic for three years. I was given a thorough examination including an EKG, and several kinds of pills for my cough and possible angina attacks. When I tried to pay, the doctor drew back and said with indignation, "You are now in a Socialist Republic where medical care is free." I was impressed.

The Rector suggested that I spend my two weekends at a hotel on the coast, since there wasn't much to do in Titograd. The University furnished a driver, who owned a taxi of his own. We were put up in the St. Stephens Hotel, a new, elegant place with its own swimming pool and marvelous views. The total cost was $9.00 per day with three good meals included. The Government owns all hotels and keeps the price low so that the poor people can afford to travel. On the second weekend, Mr. Kalmia, the computer man from UNESCO, and I rented a car and drove from St. Stephens to Dubrovnic, some sixty miles up the coast. It was Easter Sunday and many people were out in their native costumes. We walked the wall of Dubrovnic, and at one point came upon a basketball court with a game in full tilt on Easter morning! Across the road from the St. Stephens Hotel was an old monastery, within which we discovered a library and a young man studying for the priesthood. (This is the area that was hit by a recent earthquake--spring 1979.)

Our driver on both trips to the coast was a young man with a good command of English. He told us he was studying to be a hotel manager. When we asked him why he did this, because he could make so much more money driving a taxi, he informed us with great dignity that he could serve his country better as a hotel manager than he could driving a taxi. We were impressed.

Each major subject taught in the Faculties had a course labeled "Introduction to Marxist Economics, etc." but other than that I saw no evidence of communism within the University. Of course, since I didn't speak or read Serbo-Croatian, I probably didn't learn much about the realities, but I did leave with the feeling that communism rests lightly on the University people.

I roamed around freely in the city, taking as many pictures as I wished. In fact, I discovered an abandoned mosque in an old part of the city, with narrow alley streets and minimal housing and multitudes of children, all of whom wanted their pictures taken. I obliged. I did have to leave my passport at the hotels, and I assume I was registered with

the police--probably for my own protection. It did seem
strange that we were not invited into any of the homes of the
faculty, as is customary in most countries, but we were gen-
erously entertained in public restaurants.

Prices for most items purchased in stores seemed to
be low, and there were plenty of choices except for large
household items like stoves, refrigerators, and plumbing fixtures. Agriculture in the valley around Titograd was mechanized, but up in the hills there were many small bathtub-
size fields carved out of the hillsides, very much as in Greece.

On the road to St. Stephens one could, at one point,
look down into Albania. Our driver said that no one dared
go there and remarked that Albanians were strange people.

It was difficult to make plane reservations from Titograd to Belgrade, for reasons I never understood; and once
one got on the plane, as soon as it left the ground everyone--
and I mean everyone except me--lit up a cigarette. The
plane's ventilation system couldn't handle the fumes and by
the time we reached Belgrade I had a splitting headache.
There was no "no smoking" section.

I did not discuss politics or what would happen after
Tito dies with anyone while I was there. I saw no English-
language newspapers on the stands, and I have no idea what
was in their papers.

As I left Yugoslavia my feelings about the people and
the country were enthusiastically favorable. If only they could
get hold of more hard currency there would be no holding them
back. To be sure, I was in only one of the six Republics,
and the one with the least wealth, but if that one is typical
of the rest the future looks bright. I left wishing I could go
back and spend more time there.

Several Libraries in Mexico

In 1973 Lic. Ario Garza Mercado invited me to come to Mexico to help plan El Colegio de Mexico's proposed library. The
planning took several years and involved four or five trips to
Mexico from 1974 on. The Ford Foundation paid my expenses.

El Colegio de Mexico was founded by the Mexican

Federal Government to honor the anti-Franco exiled intellec-
tuals who fled to Mexico during Spain's civil war.   It is a
small, high quality, upper divisional and graduate school institution with about 200 students, limiting itself to six subject
fields--Economics, Demography, Latin American History,
Literature, Oriental Studies and Political Science.

The faculty are all on a full-time basis and therefore
do not have to work outside to make a living.   The students,
too, are on a full-time basis, with scholarships paid by the
government, and may not work outside.   Competition for admission is high and students who don't keep up with the pace
are replaced.   It's a kind if Princeton-Institute-for-Advanced-
Study-institution for the subject areas it covers.   There are
no programs for the fine arts or the sciences.

The Institution occupied temporary quarters in downtown Mexico City until its new campus south of Mexico City
was finished in 1978.

Its library collection is the strongest in Mexico for
the areas it covers--some 600,000 volumes.

El Colegio held an architectural competition limited to
four firms.   The program, which I helped draft, was given
to the firms for study.   In preparation for writing the program I visited the University of the Americas Library in
Puebla and the Agricultural University Library in Chapingo.
Both were new buildings.

The results of the competition were inconclusive.   The
plans of two firms were rejected outright.   The third firm did
a fine library but an unacceptable academic structure.   The
fourth firm was just the opposite.   Finally the College gave
the contract to Teodoro Gonzales de Leon, a poetic and highly
imaginative architect.   The plans went through many versions
before Senor Garza and I were satisfied, but the end results
are quite good.   The total campus structure, of which the library is one wing on three levels, is exceedingly beautiful.
It was constructed on an old lava bed and the architects were
careful to retain rock outcroppings and trees as much as possible.

Purchasing furniture and equipment for the project was
unsatisfactory because Mexico does not like to import anything
that can be made at home--a foreign exchange problem.   But
there is no Mexican company that specializes in library equip-

ment and furniture. The Federal Government maintains a
department that manufactures some library equipment, but
it made no bracket-type book shelving. The department did
agree to follow our specifications and to manufacture bracket
shelving. They got it almost right. They also designed and
made several types of tables and carrels, which came out
pretty well. For photographs, see Ario Garza Mercado's
new book, Function y Forma de la Biblioteca Universitaria.
Working with the Mexican librarians, architects and engineers
was easy, interesting and great fun, always. Although I could
speak very little Spanish I could understand most of what they
said and could read Spanish easily. Their sense of humor,
their hospitality, and their intelligence place them at the top
of all the people I have worked with, including us gringos.
Contrary to our stereotypes, they do work hard, but they get
so much fun out of each other as they work. They seem to
know how to mix work with living far better than we do.

For example, because of the time schedule for constructing the new structure the crews worked several shifts
twenty-four hours per day, and everyone on the job seemed
to be working at top speed. As the project neared completion, Lic. Jose Louis Castillo Tufino, the engineer in charge
of the project, decided to give a party for everyone involved
with the project. I was invited, and of course flew down.
The party began on the site about 1:30 p. m. Pots of various
kinds of sauces and food were cooking away with tantalizing
smells coming out of each. There was plenty of liquor available. Tortillas and tacos with at least a dozen kinds of fill-
ings were served for engineers, bosses, workmen and others.
Mexicans are great raconteurs, and as the drinking continued
the tales became longer and more dramatic, each person acting out his story. It wasn't hard to follow the plot even
though one didn't understand all the language.

Finally, about 3:30, barbecued sheep were put on the
table and the serious eating began. The kinds of Mexican
foods we get in our chain restaurants in the United States
with their simplistic seasonings bear little resemblance to the
highly sophisticated and subtly seasoned food we had to eat
that day. I left about 6 p. m. because I had to go back to
my hotel to rest for a dinner party that was to begin at 10:00.
The rest of the people were going strong when I left. The
next day everyone was back to work at 8:00 a. m., bright and
cheerful as ever.

Another example: I usually stayed at the Luma Hotel

while working on the project, but on one trip I stayed at a
different hotel, at the suggestion of my host. During the
night some small creatures kept biting me and I didn't get
much sleep. In the morning I complained to my host and he
replied, "Well, what did you expect us to provide--lions?"

The only project I ever worked on with an architect
who got his drawings completely right the first time around--
Senor Carlos Hernando Brito--was on the library for the Department of Horticulture (which has a graduate program with
over one hundred students). But this building was never constructed because of the change of Presidents in 1976; a new
Director decided that the department didn't need a library.

Another project I worked on was for the rapidly growing Autonoma Metropolitana Universidad at Iztapolapa, now
under construction; and another, for the Institute for Electrical Researches in Cuernavaca, is still in the planning
stage, as of March 1979.

MY SABBATICAL YEAR PROJECT 1969-70

I decided to photograph a representative group of new library buildings in the United States, Canada, Great Britain and western Europe that were generally considered by librarians and architects to be successful buildings. To select these buildings I wrote friends whose judgment I trusted. The Educational Facilities Laboratories, Inc. gave me a grant for the project, and shared the cost of publishing the resulting book with the Council on Library Resources. I traveled in the United States by car and plane, and abroad by plane and train. Except for a breakdown in equipment in Pittsburgh, and for being marooned by snowstorms in the Midwest, there were no unusual or especially interesting episodes on the trips.

During the entire project, only one librarian, the Law Librarian of Oxford University, refused to let me photograph his or her library. Everyone else, here and abroad, was gracious and helpful. I did learn, early in my travels, that if I were to keep to a schedule it was better to arrive unannounced. Otherwise my friends were likely to throw a party, call a staff meeting, or ask me to speak to a seminar. Librarians everywhere are hospitable people.

Even though I tried to keep records of each photograph taken, when it came to listing them in my book, I did make mistakes, expecially for the libraries in Southern France-- Aix-en-Provence, Marseilles, and Nice Universities. And although I did not go to Finland, I asked a friend to photograph one special library I was interested in. Something went wrong and she got in the wrong library and the photographs were, of course, mislabeled.

The resulting book (Academic Library Buildings: Architectural Issues and Solutions), when used as it is supposed to be used--as a guide book to libraries--has apparently been helpful (at least so many have told me) to people who are beginning the planning process, and who want to know where to go to see how specific problems have been solved. The book wasn't intended to be read as a novel!

CONSULTING WORK IN THE UNITED STATES

It has been my good fortune to be asked to help as a consultant on library buildings in most states of the Union and in
one province of Canada. These libraries varied in size and
character, and no two of them were ever alike. I have enjoyed working on most of the projects, but the ones that have
been the most fun have been those where I worked with the
Sisters in Roman Catholic Women's colleges. I have tended
to concentrate on college and small university libraries because they are more interesting to me and involve less drudg-
ery, but I have worked on a few large ones, such as Utah
University, the University of Iowa, Washington University and
San Diego State University. Remodeling and enlarging buildings has been the most challenging of all because each project is like trying to solve a mystery story. There is usually one key element which, if you can identify it, makes all
the other elements fall into place. For example, at Morning-
side College, the key element was a matter of changing the
entrance level; at the Kansas University project it was a
matter of tearing out one of the three stack units and floor-
ing it over at the reading room level.

It has been my experience that in a remodeling project
the librarians who have been working in the building for some
time can seldom see what ought to be done. This was true
in my own case at Colorado when the 1965 addition was being
planned. Fortunately I recognized the symptoms and called
in Keyes Metcalf and Robert A. Miller to set my thinking
straight.

Consulting on a remodeling job is quite different from
working on a new building. Deciding whether the consultant
should confine his efforts to helping write the program, leav-
ing it to the architect to find the solutions, or whether the
consultant should try to conceive the total solution that would
make a good workable library isn't always a black and white
issue, as some consultants have claimed. It depends on who
the consultants and architects are. And even if the consultant follows the last course, he would normally propose his

suggestions in such a way that the architect has full opportunity to work his magic.   A good program should tell the
architect everything he ought to know about the purposes of
a library, but even so, it is sometimes easier for an expe-
rienced consultant to visualize the possibilities in an existing
building than it is for the architect.   In any case, it really
doesn't matter where the suggestions come from if the working relations among the planning team are right.

Most of the remodeling projects with which I have been
involved have come out reasonably well, but not all of them.
The Rice University project had so many sacred cows that
had to be appeased from a political point of view that a
straight-forward solution wasn't possible.   The end result
was not too good.

The same degree of success with new buildings has
pretty much been true.   The California State University at
Chico project failure was probably my fault because I did not
know what the state planning officials expected of me.   And
the Temple University first floor layout didn't come out right,
I think because I trusted the architect too fully.   On one of
the Texas University projects I found myself agreeing with
the Librarian in opposition to the architect, and since the
University president was committed to backing the architect,
the librarian resigned and my services were no longer needed.
On most projects there have had to be minor compromises
that neither the architect nor the consultant liked.   I guess
the point is that in judging the success of a building one can't
be certain that the mistakes one sees are the fault of the librarian, the consultant, the architect, the administration--or
the donor.   The California Institute of Technology tower design was, so I was told, forced on the Institute by the donor.
I would hate to think any of the other parties involved was
to blame.

Things that Shouldn't Happen to a Consultant

Sometimes the problems one encounters as a consultant have
little to do with knowledge of building problems.   For example, in a few cases the president has indicated, although
always in an indirect and discreet manner, his lack of con-
fidence in his librarian and he has wanted me to confirm his
judgment.   I have always tried to avoid this responsibility,
but not always successfully.   Usually when this problem exists,

it is because of the librarian's inability to communicate, rather than a lack of intelligence or ability. This situation is always embarrassing, especially when I have found that the fault lies with the president, not the librarian. Presidents don't usually take kindly to such advice. But even in those cases where it seemed to me the president was right, the librarian, either in a new position or with different responsibilities in his own institution, has found greater happiness and satisfaction in his or her work.

The University of Pittsburgh Consultation

In the late 1940s A. L. Robinson, a distinguished member of the Pittsburgh Chemistry Department serving as Director of Libraries, asked me to spend a week studying Pittsburgh's library building problem. I looked forward with considerable pleasure to this task for a very special reason, which was that Rufus H. Fitzgerald, then Chancellor of the University, and his predecessor, who had conceived and promoted the "Cathedral of Learning" plan, had both been on the staff of the University of Iowa. I had hopes that I could continue the Iowa tradition at Pitt.

At that time, the University Library in the Cathedral of Learning tower was occupying several levels, accessible only by elevator. Both students and faculty of the University expressed irritation over the time required to get to and from the library. After measuring these delays I became convinced there was indeed a serious problem, and one that could be cured only by moving the library out of the tower into a separate building that would have a more horizontal expression.

The library also faced a problem of expansion. Space on levels immediately above and below the library was not available. Separating the library by several levels in the tower would complicate an already confused plan. Furthermore, the amount of floor space on each level was so small that a sensible layout of library operations was impossible -- the same problem that the California Institute of Technology has faced in its tower library.

So, in making my report, the first and most important recommendation was that the University should move the library out of the tower into a separate building that could be massed in a manner that would permit efficiency and convenience for both users and staff.

To say that all hell broke loose when my report reached the Chancellor's desk would not be appropriate because the Chancellor was a religious man, but the central administration was not pleased. Robinson and the librarians were of course delighted. I was thanked formally and my fee was paid, but it was clear to me that I had broken the Iowa connection. I went home in disgrace, but sure in my own mind that I had made the right recommendations.

Although I had no further communication with the University Administration, I learned that the University did decide to follow my suggestions and the Hillman Memorial Library was constructed, without my help of course. Consultants learn that they must expect a certain percentage of their rewards in heaven.

Many years later, in 1974, El Colegio de Mexico requested the Ford Foundation to pay the costs of a consultant. The Foundation consented and I was chosen to be the consultant. John Funari, then head of the Ford Foundation Office in Mexico City, welcomed me with a tale of his part in the Pitt library project. As a member of the Administrative staff at Pitt he was given the assignment of carrying out my recommendations--apparently not long after I had made them. He was, of course, very discreet in not revealing the process of making the decision to move the library out of the tower, but he made it clear that it took some doing. I have always assumed that A. L. Robinson's sweet reasonableness was a major factor. At any rate, the library was moved and Pitt now has the Hillman Library. As a precaution, if I do go to heaven, I will be careful to avoid meeting the two Chancellors of the University. Incidentally, I was not invited to the Hillman dedication ceremony.

Wyoming. The University of Wyoming

At the University of Wyoming, in addition to the usual reviewing of the plans, I was asked to meet with the University Trustees, who were dubious about the size of the proposed building. We were able to sidetrack their interest in this issue by getting them into a discussion of whether exterior doors should open inward or outward, or whether revolving doors would be better. In Laramie the winds blow very hard much of the time, and getting in and out of doors is an important matter. By the time the Trustees had argued this question for an hour or so, they had lost interest in the main issue, and approved the plans. But not before they made a passing swipe by reducing the size of the offices of the American Studies Program, which were to be located in the library.

California State Colleges

Charles Luckman, of Lever Brothers soap company fame before he became a well-known West Coast architect, was, at the time I was serving as consultant for Los Angeles State College, a member of the State College Board of Trustees. He had been opposing the sensible, rectangular-shaped addition to the library and was advocating a tower type of structure, which he thought would be highly visible as a symbol of the College from the San Bernardino Freeway. A battle between him and the College was shaping up for the meeting with the Board at which the plans would be voted upon.

In defense of our plans, Mr. William Eshelman, the Director of Libraries, presented letters from librarians who had had experience with tower libraries. I explained the many disadvantages of tower libraries. My explanation infuriated Mr. Luckman who stated, among other things, in his dramatic manner, that he would not approve any "blockbuster" libraries. At this point I think he sensed that he was going to be on the losing side of the Board vote, because he announced that he would refrain from voting on the library plans. The Board approved them.

Incidentally, I was the first library consultant to be used by the Board of Trustees, or the Chancellor's Office. They must have liked the idea because I was asked later to help on the plans for San Diego State, Chico State, San Fernando Valley State and Sonoma State. I never encountered Mr. Luckman again.

Wells College, Aurora, New York

In my preliminary discussions with the President of Wells, the main issue was the selection of an architect. It was clear that the President wanted an architect who would design a dramatic, showpiece kind of building, even though it seemed

to me, after studying its problem, that the College's future
might call for considerable change in the library's size and
usage, and that this kind of future role would not be consistent with the kind of building the President had in mind. I
thought that Walter Netsch was the right architect for the
kind of building the President wanted. And Walter did the
building. I was not asked to participate in the planning, which
was proper because I would have opposed the kind of building
the College built.

Oberlin College, Ohio

Perhaps my disappointment with the outcome of the Oberlin
College Mudd Learning Center project prevents me from being
entirely objective in my feeling about that library. I should
begin by saying that both Keyes Metcalf and I are Oberlin
graduates, both with deep pride in the library's collections
and in the College itself. Keyes, with his connections with
the Azariah Root family, has had very close and deep ties
with the development of the Oberlin library, and I am sure
he would like to have had more influence in the Mudd project.
Nevertheless. . .

President Carr first asked me to help him decide
whether to remodel and enlarge the old Carnegie Library or
to build a new building, or to split the collections between
the two buildings. I wrote a long report in which I strongly
urged the College to abandon the old building and to build a
new central library. This policy was accepted.

Next came the question of the selection of an architect.
Both Keyes and I felt that Oberlin shouldn't spend more than
four and one-half or five million dollars on a structure, and
that the spirit of the building should be consistent with Oberlin's tradition of rather austere "learning and labor." My
candidate for this kind of library was Murphy and Mackey,
but the contract was given to a different architect.

The project was characterized by misunderstandings
and delays from the beginning to the end, caused mostly, in
my opinion, by the way the President handled the project, although in all fairness it must be said that at Oberlin everybody has to have a hand in everything and no one really is
boss. Early versions of the plans weren't very good and each
version seemed to become more unsatisfactory. Part of the

trouble was that the College couldn't make up its mind whether to include a computer center in the library or to leave it in the old building. The architects seemed to have trouble getting clear signals from the College.

Finally, at the 1967 San Francisco A.L.A. Conference, an architect from the firm brought out plans that were the worst they had done, and I blew my top. I was not involved in the planning from that time on.

But somewhat later I was asked by President Carr to meet with the Trustees' building committee, to advise them on whether they should go ahead and build the eleven-million dollar building the architects had proposed or should fire the architects and start all over again.

I felt, and said so, that the architects should not have designed such an expensive structure, but that inflation would eat up whatever saving might be made by starting anew with another architect. The discussion was pretty heated, and I recall at one point telling Mr. P_____, who had just given the College a large sum of money for a physical education building, that if he had the right attitude he would be giving his money toward the library instead of toward athletics. I doubt if my comments helped any. At any rate, Oberlin decided to go ahead with the project. They are still much in debt on the library. There have been two presidents involved since that time.

And then, as a final blow, Oberlin, with its reputation for integrity and lean honesty, had to call the library a "Learning Center."

Mount St. Scholastica, Atchison, Kansas

For pure joy, the Mount St. Scholastica Library was the most fun of any of my projects. The Sisters were so pleasant, so able, and so easy to work with. Their sense of humor made every hour a pleasant one. At that time the Sisters were not allowed to eat in the same room with men, so when I ate there I ate in solemn splendor, all alone in an elegant dining room, while the Sister Librarian stood in the doorway and visited with me. That restriction has since been changed. Joseph Murphy, the architect on that project, felt the same way I did about the Sisters, and as a result he outdid himself in seeing that they got a fine building.

ASSOCIATING WITH LIBRARY ASSOCIATIONS

Although I am not unmindful of the old adage about fools who
rush in where angels fear to tread, I should not, nor do I
wish to, avoid writing about my working experiences with ALA
and other library associations. ALA and all the other library
organizations and associations are under constant evaluation--
internal and external. In judging these associations one of the
kinds of evidence that should be considered is the feelings and
attitudes of working librarians toward them over a long period
of time. The trouble is that few librarians have recorded
their personal feelings and thus there is a lack of evidence of
this type. I hope my comments will be a beginning supply.
It is true of course that the discussions of the ALA Council
meetings and other boards are useful evidence, but they are
not the same as considered personal testimony.

For reasons I shall explain later, it is more difficult
to discuss one's relations to ALA in retrospect than it is to
the other organizations I have been involved with: the Colorado Library Association, the Iowa Library Association, the
Association of College & Research Libraries, the Association
of Research Libraries, the Human Relations Area files and
the Center for Research Libraries. This is because ALA,
in a way, is a huge carnival with so many side shows one
has trouble identifying the main show, let alone deciding
whether it or the side shows are more important at any one
time.

My qualifications for recording my experiences seem
adequate: I served on the ALA Executive Board (1946-1950)
at a crucial time in the history of ALA--Carl Milam's retirement years--and on many ALA committees, including the Intellectual Freedom Committee at the time the Library Bill of
Rights was being written, and the ALA 75th Anniversary Celebration Committee. I ran for ALA President once and was
defeated. I served as President of ACRL two terms, 1951
and 1961, years in which ACRL came close to withdrawing
from ALA, and on many ACRL committees. For two years
I chaired a committee that stood off an attempt by the Amer-

ican Bar Association to force universities to administer their
law libraries separately from the General library--even if
they did not want to do so (1958-60).   As President of ACRL
I started the Committee on Resources.

    In the Association of Research Libraries I served one
term on its executive board (1951-54) and was chairman of
the Committee that created the ARL-University Microfilms
plan for publishing doctoral dissertations in microform, and
of the joint ARL-ALA Committee on the National Union Catalog.

    I was President of the Colorado Library Association
for three terms, 1937, 1938, and 1964.   I was a member of
the Cooperative Committee for planning large university libraries from its beginning and was chairman in 1948.   I was
a member of the committee that drafted the organization char-
ter for the Midwest Inter Library Center (now the Center for
Research Libraries) and was chairman of its Executive Board,
1944-1945.

    I was President of the University of Iowa chapter of
the American Association of University Professors in 1945
and President of the Iowa State AAUP Conference in 1946.   I
served on the Board of Directors of the Human Relations Area
Files, Inc., from 1958-1972, and one term on its executive
board.   I was chairman of a state-wide committee in Colorado
that organized the Colorado Associated University Press in
1965--one of the early joint university presses in the U.S..

    So much for my qualifications and points of contact
with library and related associations.   Now for some comments on each of these.

American Library Association

ALA is an easy target for cynical remarks, and I have con-
tributed my share--wheels within wheels, motion for the sake
of motion, etc.--hundreds of committees that work hard on
issues that (like a Western desert rain cloud that sends down
water that never reaches the ground) have no effect on the
activities of working librarians.

    In terms of real changes that have been made in the
last twenty-five years in the activities of American librarians,

one can make a strong case that ALA has been less responsible than have been other organizations and individuals.   Exceptions obviously have to be conceded in ALA's favor in the
case of intellectual freedom and censorship in libraries and
in federal aid for libraries.   And to another function less
tangible but possibly quite important--as I shall discuss later.

In defense of my claim I would start by saying that in
the field of library education, ALA fought the establishment
of the University of Chicago Graduate Library School--the
school that has had more influence on raising standards in
library schools than has anything ALA has done.   And to its
discredit, ALA has allowed the proliferation of library schools
to the point where they are a national disgrace in terms of
quality.

I argue that at least for academic librarians, Archi-
bald MacLeish provided leadership that had more to do with
salary levels throughout the country than anything ALA has
done in the last thirty years.   He did this by immediately
raising the salaries of the Library of Congress staff and by
speaking up in their defense.   He also appointed high quality
staff members--such as Luther Evans and Fred Wagman.

Leadership in the electronic communication revolution
now occuring in libraries has been coming not from ALA but
from individuals like Frederick Kilgour and library directors
like Herman Fussler at Chicago, and in other libraries and
library schools like Stanford, Pittsburgh and Harvard.

Leadership in the architectural changes that have oc-
curred--especially in academic libraries--came not from ALA
committees but from the self appointed Cooperative Committee
on Large University Libraries Planning and from the Educational Facilities Laboratories, Inc. in the 1950s.   Leadership in the centralized cataloging movement came not from
the dreary ALA committees on cataloging and classification
but from the Association of Research Libraries working closely with officials at the Library of Congress.

And so one could go on with other examples.

But, as I mentioned earlier, these examples, in some
ways, miss the point of the value of ALA to librarians.

There is wisdom and understanding in the comments
that the late Robert Lester (then Secretary of the Carnegie
Corporation) made to E. W. MacDiarmid and me as we sat

in the peacock alley of the Drake Hotel at an ALA Midwinter meeting, watching the parade go by--mostly female. Mr. Lester's comments were somewhat as follows (after I had made some crack about how silly it was for those underpaid librarians to waste their time and money coming to an annual ALA conference):

> Yes, but you must understand that the ALA meetings are a kind of religious experience to them. At home they work hard, are underrewarded, not appreciated, and they feel they aren't getting anywhere. They come here in the spirit of a religious pilgrimage. They pay 25¢ for a cup of coffee, and they listen to the big shots and they decide things in their committee meetings, and they feel they have done things. The process becomes of importance in itself. (I cited this statement before in an article "Library Associations in America," Library Quarterly XXXI, no. 4 (1961) p. 383).

And, he reminded us, that participating in ALA committees and Council debates was one of the best ways for young librarians to make themselves known, and thus get ahead in the profession. I offer a couple examples of the wisdom of Mr. Lester's remarks. Just prior to our entry into WWII, when President Roosevelt was trying to persuade Americans to help Britain survive, Carl Milam asked me (I don't recall why I was on the stage at the time) to present a resolution at a Midwinter meeting offering ALA's backing to an Act Roosevelt was trying to get through Congress, backing aid to Britain. The resolution was debated at some length and eventually passed. Obviously this had nothing to do with the working activities of the members of the audience, nor with the passage of the Act in Congress. But it surely was good to be a member of an organization that cared about issues of national importance. It made me proud of ALA, and I think many others felt the same way. It is interesting that Carl Milam was keeping close track of matters of this kind.

Another example is the actions of ALA's members concerning equal treatment of the races--as expressed by a last-minute shift in an annual meeting place. The conference was moved from a Southern city that wouldn't accept blacks in the hotels to Washington D. C., where blacks were accepted as equals. Again, this action made me proud of ALA.

On the negative side, there are too many instances

where ALA members have cringed at the stupidity and lack
of vision in the Association Establishment. Perhaps the best
example of this was when Milton Ferguson as President of
ALA led an intemperate attack on the appointment of Archi-
bald MacLeish as Librarian of Congress on the grounds that
MacLeish was not a trained librarian and that he lacked experience in the library field. It was the low quality of Ferguson's attack that bothered many. (I even was guilty of
writing a letter to Library Journal saying that a poet didn't
seem likely to have the qualities a librarian needed.) By the
time Mr. MacLeish retired as Librarian of Congress to go to
the State Department on a war assignment, he compiled a
record that made him one of the best Librarians of Congress
we have had.

Another example is the ALA opposition to the kind of
work the University of Chicago Graduate Library School intended to engage in. The Waples-Thompson debate typified
this opposition with Thompson taking the ALA position.

And so, there are the two sides to ALA: one as a
kind of Church for the Religion of Librarianship, and one as
a big loosely knit bureaucracy frequently making errors in
judgment on library matters, but sometimes taking positions
and promoting causes that make its members proud.

My first ALA committee was on the ALA committee
on library buildings, in 1940. At that time this committee
tried to represent all types of libraries. I, promptly, with
the backing of William Jesse and one or two others, objected
to this inclusiveness and began to argue for a separate committee for academic libraries. The following year the separation was made and academic libraries had their own committee within ACRL.

My term on the ALA Executive Board, 1946-1950, was
a turbulent one. I brought to the board a negative, anti-ALA
attitude I had acquired as early as 1931 when I started reading Library Quarterly, and after the Waples-Thompson de -
bates. My studies at the GLS revealed even more clearly
to me the lack of scholarship in the profession and the high
degree of emotionalism governing the association's official
actions. I was a pain in the neck to Carl Milam and the
ALA staff. Milam once told me he wished he could turn me
over his knee and paddle me because I kept complaining about
the state of membership records and about almost everything
the headquarters staff was doing. ALA was run almost like
a family with Carl as the stern and dominating Father.

In retrospect, even though we complainers were right about the state of the headquarters work, it is clear the Mr. Milan had been doing a good job of trying to guide a profession that was approaching the end of an era without realizing it. It is fair to say that he paid too little attention to minor headquarters matters and that perhaps he did listen too much to a small group of Establishment-minded friends of his generation.

The fiasco of Milam's allowing himself to be persuaded to run for the Presidency of ALA at the time of his retirement was symptomatic of what was wrong with ALA. Dean E. W. MacDiarmid was President of ALA that year. He and I, as was our habit, were rooming together at ALA Conferences and I could see how an unorganized but nevertheless tightly knit group of elder statesmen threw a blanket of influence around Mr. Milam. Not only was Milam insulated from the ALA membership, but so was Dean MacDiarmid and the other officers. Even I could see that there was widespread resentment against Mr. Milam's running. I tried to tell this to MacDiarmid, but he didn't believe me. The election was unimportant in itself, because ordinarily it doesn't matter at all who the ALA President is, but what made this one important was that it was a lousy way to recognize, at his retirement, the very real and important accomplishments of Mr. Milam.

The Executive Board gave a retirement dinner for Milam and it was my privilege and pleasure to select and present him with a fine fly rod, a line, and a good selection of flies--which he used many times afterwards.

At that time the Executive Board struggled long and hard (a whole week) to allocate the Association's budget over as many worthy projects as possible. It always was a losing battle, but each of us acquired an intimate knowledge of the work of the association. At the end of the week we gave up and told Mr. Milam he'd have to find some way to balance the budget, and he always did. The financial records were in such a state that no one knew exactly where the balance stood, so I suspect there was always plenty of leeway for Milam to play with.

Perhaps the only really important action we took was to appoint John Cory as the new Executive Secretary. John did good work in helping the profession begin to adjust itself to a new era, an era characterized by activism, library ex-

pansion and closer attention to a scholarly approach to its
problems.

At the time I was first elected to the Presidency of
The Association of College and Research Libraries, I was
pretty well convinced that academic libraries were getting the
short end of ALA's budget stick and that it was a waste of
talent to have the divisional secretaries located at the ALA
headquarters, rather than in real libraries, where the officers
would have close contact with real library problems.

Many of us in ACRL were pushing the Federation concept for ALA, a plan that was favored by Milton Lord, then
president of ALA. We were arguing that ACRL should withdraw from ALA, and we came close to bringing it off--at
least we got a clear vote of favor from the Executive Board
of ACRL. Blanche McCrum was President of ACRL and she
was in favor of secession. Charles Brown--one of the elder
statesmen in ALA as well as in ACRL--was on our side. But
at the last moment some of Charles' old friends in ALA got
to him and pleaded with him not to break up the good old
ALA. Charles was a very emotional man and the appeals of
his lifelong friends won him over to their side. Without his
vote on the Executive Board we never had a chance. We lost.

But if we had won, ALA would probably have been
forced to adopt the federation concept and today it would be
a true national spokesman for all the library interests in the
country--the law librarians, the Special Librarians, etc. Although each constituent division would control its own budget,
publishing programs, and officers, funds were to be alloted
to the central ALA to work on the issues that are of national
and common concern to all kinds of librarians--academic
freedom, censorship, Federal aid, leadership in the electronic
communication revolution and so on. Many librarians today
wish we rebels in ACRL had won our fight.

In 1961 when I was again elected to the presidency of
ACRL I think the membership expected me to lead another
fight for ACRL independence. I tried but I simply didn't know
how to direct a campaign that would win. Frank Lundy, director of the University of Nebraska Libraries, warned me
that I was making the fight too much of a one-man show. I
admitted that he was right, but I didn't have the time or energy or the drive to do what was needed.

One of the ACRL projects that I led with some success

was chairing the committee appointed to put a stop to John Hervey's attempt (as spokesman for the American Bar Association) to make it impossible for Universities, if they wished to do so, to administer law libraries as part of the university's central library system. I worked closely with William K. Selden (executive director of the National Commission on Accrediting) who was trying to persuade the national associations to use sensible accrediting programs. (This project has been described in two published articles--the one on "Library Associations in America" cited earlier in the chapter, and "The Government of Law Libraries," Law Library Journal, November 1960, p. 461-68).

During the discussions I was invited to meet with Dr. Selden and members of the American Bar Association's Council on Legal Education in the main dining room of the Washington Hotel in Washington. After a couple of martinis the arguments became heated and loud and the dining room staff became concerned. The maitre d' skillfully got us out of the room into a small room where we could shout at each other harmlessly. Later, at a meeting of the Law Library Association in Minneapolis, the basic issue was discussed fully (and quietly) by Mr. Hervey, Dr. Selden, and myself. It was generally agreed by the law librarians present that on the basis of fact, logic, and good principles Dr. Selden and I made Mr. Hervey look silly, but he merely smiled pleasantly and ignored us, knowing as he did that the American Bar Association had the political power to do as it pleased, and that they need pay no attention to us librarians, or even to the National Commission on Accrediting. Mr. Hervey never made a public withdrawal of his previous threat, but in practice he never, to my knowledge, tried to enforce it.

Association of Research Libraries

Working in the Association of Research Libraries was quite different from working with ALA. ARL was small enough and made up of libraries that were sufficiently alike in size and purpose so that committee recommendations had a good chance of being adopted and put into practice without a lot of time wasted in procedure. For example, the work I did as Chairman of the Committee on Publishing Doctoral Dissertations (described elsewhere in this volume) took not more than a year in committee study, and once it was adopted by ARL it was put into practice immediately (even though it took several years for the committee to implement the plan fully).

The manner in which the joint ARL-ALA Committee on the National Union Catalog was set up illustrates the difference between the two organizations. At the time this committee was established in ARL, our group was suspicious of the potential trouble ALA would cause through its red tape and cumbersome procedures. So we made it clear that if ALA tried to obstruct the work of the committee, we would go underground and come up as a purely ARL committee, even though we knew we needed the umbrella coverage of ALA for legal contract work. There were a couple of times when we had to use that threat, but in each case ALA backed away. It was during this time that the contract was let for the pre-1955 imprints segment of the National Union Catalog--the largest bibliographic project ever undertaken. Without the intelligent leadership of John Cronin, William Welsh, and John Dewton and others at the Library of Congress this project would never have been possible.

Now that ARL has enlarged its membership to the point beyond which its decisions can be made by a manageable number of librarians whose needs and problems are so much alike that decisions come easily, the main function of the association may change. Like ACRL, its main function may be to dispense information, not take action on the basis of committee reports.

But perhaps in all library associations the days for taking action will have to be suspended until the effects of the electronic communication revolution are more fully understood. As readers of the September 15th (1978) issue of Library Journal will realize, there will be policy decisions that associations will have to make that will determine the fate of libraries, but these cannot be made until we know how to use the new technology either as part of, or in place of our existing systems. As John Berry says in his editorial, the battle must rage in the White House Conference, in the library journals, in the association debates, but the final word may come from the laboratories of IBM and other electronic scientists.

And More...

In comparison with ALA, ACRL and ARL, the state library associations I have been involved with have not had much influence on national library policies, or even policies within their states. But they have, nevertheless, been equally important, as well as great fun. It was in the Colorado Library Association that I learned to try out my wings with minor committee assignments and in debates on the floor of general sessions. Here one meets in an informal and relaxed setting real librarians--the ones that do the work in libraries--not just the top administrators, who get their expenses paid to the national meetings and who probably would be incapable of doing the daily work of any department in their library.

Other library-related associations that I have worked with have been interesting as a basis for comparison with the library associations. For example the Human Relations Area Files, Inc. Herman Fussler once characterized the HRAF as the most expensive bibliographic boondoggle ever conceived by man, and in a way he was right. The usefulness of the Files to social scientists, even those not working in cross cultural research, is undeniable, but the cost of the Files is high, both in getting the information into the 25 sets of the Files, and also in providing the equipment needed to maintain them. As users of the Files know, the project is not only a bibliography of the activities of primitive cultures expressed by subject headings, but the actual texts of primary research materials are filed behind each subject heading. The result is great bulk. If the Files project were being organized today the bibliographic information would all come via the computer terminal, and much of the textual material would be made available in microfiche. In fact, the Files headquarters are using both of these devices today, but the great bulk of the Files are in paper form.

HRAF is governed by a board of directors made up of representatives of the 25 member institutions. Most of the directors are anthropologists, but there are always a few token librarian members. Because in most of the 25 member institutions the cost of the Files is paid from the library budget, the anthropologists think it wise to allow a few librarians on the board, even though they are considered dimwits with no real understanding of the importance of the Files. The librarians' complaints about high costs are usually ignored. The business of the board is largely budgetary, and like the ALA and ACRL boards, the HRAF board usually ends its sessions with the budget unbalanced. They then leave the matter to the President (executive secretary) to find ways of making up the differences between income and expenditures. The President of HRAF has, like the executive officers of the ALA and ACRL, been a strong person who could cope.

The HRAF board was until recently an all male board and traditionally the banquet dinners were held in Maury's with much drinking and conviviality. But when the University of Iowa sent a female director, the dinners could no longer be held in Maury's (at that time an all male place). With the shift something went out of HRAF élan!

It was most interesting for me to listen to some of the great names in anthropology engage in sharp infield fighting with their colleagues over philosophical differences on the value of cross cultural research. These men, being brighter than us librarians, used sharper knives for their battles.

A second library-related organization with which I have worked is the Center for Research Libraries (originally the Midwest Inter Library Center). The CRL was quite similar to HRAF in that its governing board consisted of a mixture of librarians and non-librarians, and in the size of the organization. There was no prototype to study when MILC was organized. The struggles involved with constructing the building have been discussed elsewhere in this volume and in Bauman's biography of Angus Snead Macdonald. However, the biggest problems we wrestled with were over philosophical differences on the scope and purposes of the Center. Two of the member institutions (Indiana and Illinois) feared that the Center might interfere with their success in making their libraries the biggest and best of their kind. The other members had shades of enthusiasm for joint financing and locating of special research collections that the Center might purchase for the use of its members. As for financing the Center, the poor member institutions felt that, like the federal income tax, the ability to pay should determine the member's contribution. The wealthy and largest members (who used the Center least) felt that the member assessments should be based on use of the center. I insisted that use should be defined not by the numbers of inquiries a member made of the Center, but also by the amount of material a member stored there. This confused the issue considerably, and at the time I left the Center to come back to the University of Colorado, the issue had not been settled. Since then (probably soon after I left!) a formula was developed that all could accept.

These and other issues resulted in lively but friendly debates in the board meetings. The non-library members of the board (most of whom were top administrators like Dean Ingraham from Wisconsin, Henry Heald from the Illinois Institute of Technology, Vice President Middlebrook from

Minnesota, and Judge Wildermuth from Indiana) were inclined to be a bit impatient over the nit-picking debates of us librarians, because the issues seemed unimportant to them. The representatives from Wayne State, Minnesota, and Wisconsin consistently took what seemed to me an enlightened and progressive point of view on the issues.

Without the skillful administrative talent of Ralph Esterquest, and later of Gordon Williams, the CRL would not have become the national facility some of us dreamed of in the early days. In fact, when one considers all of the above associations, one could generalize enough to say that without strong administrators in charge, none of these agencies would have been able to achieve the levels of importance the board members had in mind.

Another organization I worked with which has little direct relationship to libraries, the American Association of University Professors, was governed in quite a different manner. When I moved to the University of Iowa in 1943 with a strong interest in the problem of faculty governance, I found the local chapter to consist of some 17 members who gathered once in a while to whine about the low state of their salaries and the fact that their children couldn't get free tuition at the University. I made a rabble-rousing speech about what the chapter could do if it got off its duff. And so of course I was elected President next year. With the help of Professor John Gerber and a group of young turks we built the membership up to over four hundred and began agitating for restoration of the University Senate and the other organs of faculty participation in university administration. We didn't get the Senate until years later but we did get an advisory faculty committee and a willingness of the President to work more closely with the Faculty. After that year I was elected to the Presidency of the State chapter of the AAUP Conference--a more spineless organization I have never seen.

In retrospect, I shudder at the thought of the amount of time in my life that has been spent working with association committees as well as on campus committees. I'm surprised that I got anything else done. In fact, I'm not sure I did get anything else done. I do know that during most of my professional years I taught a course in bibliography and took my turn at the Reference desk evenings, but that a year or two before I retired, the Reference Librarian finally came to me and suggested in her most diplomatic and kindly manner that maybe it would be better if I spent my time and energy on association and campus committee work. And I agreed.

PUBLICATIONS SINCE 1958

The Building volume of the State-of-the-Library-Art series was a terrible bore to write (and to read) because I had to wade through a large mass of uninteresting articles and books. There wasn't one single glint of humor in the whole lot. Except for the professional obligation and the chance to visit foreign libraries, the project was an awful chore. I can't believe the resulting book was of much use to anyone.

The small book, Planning the College and University Library Building, which the Pruett Press published for me in 1960, I wrote because I knew, as a result of the consulting work I was doing, that there was a need for some guidance among the hundreds of librarians who were trying to plan new buildings. I knew that Keyes Metcalf's monumental book was four years away. In spite of the mistakes and typographical errors in the book, many librarians found the book helpful. In doing a revised edition of the book a very strange thing happened to the first issues. Apparently in 1968, while the Pruett Press was preparing the copy, the printer in charge was angry with his boss or somebody, because he deliberately mixed up several paragraphs and the book came out pretty well scrambled. All the copies that had been distributed had to be recalled. I've always been sorry that the book wasn't valuable because, if it had been, the defective copies might have become attractive to collectors. The first edition was translated and published in Spanish, and also in Japanese. The Japanese published a very attractively bound and boxed edition. I can't read the Japanese but I can admire the beauty of the binding.

The second book I wrote on the subject of school libraries, The School Library, I have never been able to decide whether to be proud or ashamed of. I did the book in part because Dr. G. R. Gottschalk, the editor of the series, flattered me by telling me I was the only person in the country who could do it, and in part because I had considerable respect for some of the men on the advisory and editorial boards--Ralph W. Tyler and John Dale Russell, for example.

The latter worked closely with me as my editor and kept me
from saying many outlandish things that probably were true
but better left unsaid.

As I reread the book now (which I had never done
before) it seems to be full of interesting insights and ideas.
The concept of the school library it advocates is an enlightened one.   But, as far as I know, the book had no impact.
I have never met anyone who has read it.

The Economics of Book Storage in College and University Libraries, published by the Association of Research
Libraries and The Scarecrow Press, Inc. , laid down the
conditions which ought to govern the process of arriving at
the decision as to whether or not a book should be stored
outside the regular stack sequences, and if so, it proposed a
way of determing the costs. I had wanted to call this book "The
Politics and Economics of Book Storage, " but I was outvoted.
There wasn't any way then, nor is there now, of proving or
disproving my contention that costs, as a factor in making
the decision, are less important than the factors of the availability of space and the effects on the work of the faculty.
Herman Fussler's studies showed what the percentage of dis-
contentment, so to speak, might be in certain fields of knowledge if some of the books were sent to storage, but they
couldn't tell one if the inconvenienced minorities might be
more important people than the majorities who were not affected.

Nor was there any fully satisfactory way of measuring
relative costs, or the durability of the various systems, for
the simple reason that except for the European Compactus
system, the other ones hadn't been in use long enough.   Also,
it does not follow that a manufacturer's costs on a past job
will be the same on a future job.   His bids may be more a
reflection of the needs in his plant than of real costs at another time or another place.

Today, many of the large universities are resorting
to storage primarily because there is no space for enlarging
their central libraries any more.   Costs and potential incon-
venience to the faculty are not the determining factors in
those cases.   However, the interplay among the three factors
might be expected to change from time to time and from
campus to campus.

The Manual I published in 1973 to go along with the

Academic Library Buildings volume was written primarily for laymen who might want a quick overview of the planning process, and also as a kind of introduction to my book of photographs.

In this book I seemed to have touched a raw nerve in some architects, because it made several very angry. And of course, Jerrold Orne found many faults in it, as is his wont. However, I have heard from many librarians who have found the manual useful in working with their faculty planning committees. The only part that offers new information in the manual was its chapter on the place of "Media" in planning libraries. But then, one doesn't expect new concepts in a manual.

The Colorado Academic Central Processing Project

Academic librarians in Colorado have been talking about various cooperative activities since 1938, but it wasn't until 1966, when a grant was received from the National Science Foundation (the application was written by Richard Dougherty), that a central processing operation was inaugurated. The project anticipated that every step in processing from ordering to delivering books ready for the shelves would be included. But because some members were unable to transfer enough book money into the budget the discounts did not live up to expectations, and the turn-around time was slower than desirable. Several members resented the project and dissension created difficulties. Eventually the heart of the project was taken out and the project was discontinued. Since this project has been described fully by Richard M. Dougherty and Joan Maier I shall not discuss it further except to say that both Dougherty and Maier worked intelligently and diligently to make the project go.

A Matter of Style

One of my ambitions since my Oberlin days has been to write persuasively. Although the bulk of my writing has been large, there have been only a few sentences that meet my standard of good style:

At the Cornell University Library dedication ceremony in 1961, I said:

> For us, the dedication of a new university library
> building is a kind of sacrament, to which the faith-
> ful come, not to be shocked by new doctrines, but
> to be reassured and comforted by a familiar re-
> assessment of the values of the scholarly life, for
> which the library is a symbol, and to be strength-
> ened by the application of academic grace to our
> humble spirits.

And then, later in the speech:

> Having taught.... in our Honors program, I know
> first hand how desperately our better students need
> something that will help them as they huddle around
> the small fires of learning discussing the meaning
> of the dangers they see in the darkness of the outer
> world.

A bit corny perhaps.

And then in my 1961 paper on "Critique of Library
Associations in America, " I concluded with the following bitter and somewhat demagogic, but nerve-touching, sentences:

> Much of the sound and fury which we mistakenly
> think of as the American Library Association would
> dry up and never be heard of again, because it is
> nothing but the clanking of the machinery of the
> Association.
> The other noises we might begin to hear would
> be the sounds of librarians--teachers, researchers,
> catalogers, reference librarians, children's librar-
> ians, administrators, documentalists, etc. --all hard
> at work. That would be the true sound of the
> American Library Association.

I should explain that in this passage I was defending
the Federation idea as the basis for A. L. A.'s reorganization,
a point for which Milton Lord, I, and many others have
argued.

RETIREMENT

All my professional life has been spent during a time when university libraries were expected to grow in size and quality as rapidly as possible. Universities were proud of their libraries and considered them to be an important asset in attracting scholars to their faculties. Library directors whose libraries did not keep up with the pace of their competitive universities were likely to lose their positions.

But in the 1960s--perhaps the beginning could be timed with the publication of John Millett's charges that librarians were packrats, sitting on huge collections of unused books-- attitudes of administrators toward their libraries began to shift.

Universities had become large and their management difficult and specialized, calling for the managerial type of president as opposed to the older scholar-administrators. Financial analysts were put on the trail of waste in the universities. It was discovered that a large percentage of the books in a university library were seldom used--something that scholars always knew and assumed to be what a research library was all about. This fact came to light at the time when research in the humanities and social sciences, which needed the large libraries, had taken a back seat to research in the sciences (the post-Sputnik period), whose research needs, to a large extent, could be met primarily from journal files. And this trend magnified the belief that the large university libraries were a luxury. Many state legislatures employed analysts who took up the hue and cry against the large libraries.

It is a little hard to understand the intense feeling against academic libraries and librarians in view of the fact that libraries seldom use more than five percent of a university's academic budget. Perhaps we librarians have brought this down on ourselves by our habit of beating our breasts in public so often. Paul Buck's rejoinder to Keyes Metcalf's pleas for economy at the ARL meeting at the Allerton House in 1957 was a convincing restatement of the reasons why a quality library was a necessity in a quality university, regardless of how many of its books stood unused at any one time.

By 1970 I was feeling that most of my energy had to be spent defending principles and values that had governed my professional life from its beginning in 1931. No matter how logical and convincing my justifications were for funds for books and space, I was not believed by my administration or by the state legislature. It was obvious that my bosses felt that my needle had gotten stuck and they were tired of the repeated cries of anguish. I felt I was hurting, not helping, the library because I was losing my battles for support.

And so in February 1972 I retired at age 64. I packed up twenty Trollope novels, and my wife and I headed for a vacation at our favorite motel in San Carlos Bay in Mexico, and we have lived happily in Boulder ever since. All the factors that make for a happy retirement have been present in our case.

I know that many people find retirement a most unhappy period in their lives. I also know there is an extensive literature on how to be happy in retirement. I intend to add only two brief comments to that literature.

First, if after all your education--formal and informal--and after a long life of varied experiences you still haven't learned to be at peace with yourself when you aren't working, then you had better look on your retirement years as a training period for whatever kind of hell you intend to encounter later. In short, if you have to worry about retirement, it's too late to do anything about it.

Second, get out of the house during the middle of the day and let your wife enjoy your absence, just as she did before you retired. I speak from my male experience, having had none as a female.

PHYSICAL INEPTITUDES

Although I have no special desire to expose my physical lim-
itations I must admit that I have special problems with cameras.   Most every camera fan forgets now and then to put
film in his camera, but I specialize in doing this in far away
places where I will never have a chance to return and cover
my mistakes.   For example, in 1968 Theda and I were priv-
ileged to spend most of a day in the Keukenhof gardens in
Holland at a time when the flowers were at their best.   It
wasn't until the next day that I discovered that my failure to
thread my camera properly caused a complete lack of pictures of the flowers.   By that time we were in England on
our way home.

And then in Saudi Arabia, as I have mentioned earlier,
the porters at the desert party allowed me to photograph
them in action--something that is never allowed in Saudi
Arabia.   Naturally, I didn't discover until later that no film
was going through the camera.

My problems with simple arithmetic also get me in
trouble.   At my son Peter's wedding, which was being held
in our house, my responsibility was to photograph the event,
with a flash attachment on my camera.   For each exposure
I had to calculate the distance and lens opening.   My daugh-
ter-in-law recalls with amusement my whispering in a loud
volume, "How much is 75 divided by 12?"   Apparently I got
the wrong answers because most of the pictures were im-
properly exposed.   Hand calculators weren't on the market
at that time.

Also, I have to confess, I have trouble following and
remembering the directions on small machines.   Each time
I plug in the flash attachment to my camera I have to go
back and read the directions to find out if the little button is
turned to X or FP.   Or to remind myself whether the wide
angle lens is 28 or 50 mm. in length.   I have several color
filters in my kit but I can never figure out which one to use.

But my worst deficiency with my camera is caused by my lack of good sense of design. It's luck, rather than skill, that causes some of my efforts to turn out well. This lack caused me real trouble in 1969 when I set out to photograph the exteriors and interiors of many academic libraries for my Academic Library Buildings book. The trouble was that my camera lens and I didn't always agree on what we saw. Lenses have no sense of romance or humor, whereas I am not always a realist when looking at a possible camera shot. I look but I don't always see. It has been suggested that I get a Brownie box camera.

However, my ineptitudes with cameras and other small machines isn't the whole story. I claim to be a very skillful fly caster and trout angler. I can tie a trout fly that my friends will buy, borrow, or steal avidly. And I did build a mountain cabin that is a joy to live in. On balance I willingly accept my condition.

SOME EXTRAS--FISHING AND THE CABIN

Many visitors think that living in Colorado, especially in
Boulder, is so exciting that it is enough recreation for anyone. But I have noticed that most Boulderites engage in one
or more of the major forms of recreation associated with
the mountains. All these major forms in Colorado are thriv-
ing today and all have undergone complete revolutions since
1931, when we first came to the state.

When we tried to buy ski harnesses in 1937, only one
store in Denver had any in stock, and these were hidden away
in a bottom drawer in the Daniels and Fishers Department
Store. And the only ski lift in Colorado was a simple rope
lift west of Denver. Camping was common but campers set
up large heavy tents and slept on the ground, wrapped in
blankets. Air mattresses and sleeping bags weren't available. Coleman lanterns and stoves may have existed, but
none was visible in our part of the state. It was World War
II, and the gear invented for Alpine warfare, that brought in
backpacking gear and chanted the whole camping scene. And,
of course, the ski industry, beginning with Aspen, has grown
into a major industry in the state, with large communities
created in the mountains.

But trout fishing in Colorado, which is my special
passion, has added so many layers of sophistication that it
has almost become an art form--if not a minor religion, or
at least a cult. Many western towns now have chapters of
Trout Unlimited which meet monthly, with paid speakers and
reports on member projects like stream restoration, anti-
dam legislation, and water conservation. These meetings
are probably better attended than are most of the churches--
except for the fringe denominations, which seem to have an
especial appeal to western ignoramuses. The professional
angling journalists make the rounds of these Trout Unlimited
meetings, spreading the message of the joys of angling, much
as do the evangelists for the churches that sponsor revival
meetings. Dave Whitlock, as one example, comes to our
meetings at least once a year, with demonstrations of his

new fly tying techniques, and his experiences fishing the
famous streams. He even conducts seminars in fly tying.

Any two trout fishermen, or fisherpersons (we haven't
quite overcome our male chauvinist terminology yet, nor have
we reached the point where we call ourselves "anglers," even
though two of our best known fishing supply stores are named
"Anglers All" and "The Western Angler") meeting on a Colorado stream wouldn't speak these days of their luck with a
Hendrickson or Tiny Blue-wing Olive fly, but would talk about
their Ephemerelle subvaria or a Pseudodocloeon anoka. An
angler must now know not only stream entomology but also
the Latin names for the insect life of each stream, and in
each of the three stages of life: nymphs, duns, and spinners.
At long last I have found a practical use for the two years
of Latin I studied at Oberlin.

A true angler, in fishing a stream new to him or her,
will first break out his insect collecting net. Meanwhile a
companion will walk upstream kicking the rocks to loosen the
insects in the stream (at the same time recording the time
of day and the temperature of the water), so that when the
angler starts to fish he will select flies that imitate those
caught in his net. This is called "matching the hatch."

Fortunately, there are short cuts for those anglers,
like me, who aren't so pure. A book called Selective Trout,
by Swisher and Richards, is our Bible. Beginning on page
122, Swisher and Richards, after years of research, have
compiled charts on the "super hatches for each section of
the country, and for the time of the year each insect is ac-
tive. These charts tell you not only which fly to use, and
when, but they also give directions for tying the flies--as
nymphs, duns or spinners. All insect names are in Latin,
of course.

To prepare for a day's fishing I now carry at least
fifty different patterns of flies in small plastic boxes, carried
in the 24 pockets on my fishing jacket (and a vest for late in
the season when it's warm), and in pouches sewn onto the
sides and top of my creel. One problem I have is that I
can't remember which box contains the fly I want. To solve
this I am compiling an index to the boxes, but I can't quite
figure out where to keep the index. And, of course, being
of sane mind and reasonable temperament, with limited time
at my disposal, in actual practice I eschew all these fifty
patterns and rely on my old favorites--Rio Grande Kings,

Grey Hackles, Hare's Ears, Renegades and Adamses. And
with these favorites I still catch my limit of trout (reduced
from 25 to six, between 1937 and 1979) if I so choose.

A true Colorado angler, in addition to his many flies,
must now carry lots of gear: a stream thermometer, a fly
threading tool, a pair of scissors, a nail clipper, a folding
wader staff, several extra spools with special lines for his
reel, a packet of various sizes of leaders, special compounds
to make his lines and flies float or sink as conditions require,
insect repellents, a rain jacket, his lunch and a flask of
bourbon to relieve his fatigue from the burden he carries.
A real pro also carries a streamside fly tying kit, in case
he encounters insects not matched in his boxes of 50. And
of course, a landing net.

The weight of this equipment has now become a problem to me in my declining years. I stagger from car to
stream (places that require a long walk between the two are
avoided) and I dare say that soon each of us gaffers will have
to hire a porter to share the burden.

All of this additional weight has created a safety problem for us anglers, because the rocks in most of our stream
beds are very slippery. The weights we now carry interfere
with our sense of balance and we fall down more often than
we used to in the old days. The danger of broken legs has
increased. Our mates, anxiously awaiting our return at the
day's end, now insist we file a stream plan, so that if we
don't return in a reasonable time, the rangers will know
where to search for our submerged and broken bodies. I
expect the insurance companies soon to publish special rates
for us anglers.

This is a far cry from fishing in Colorado in 1931.
Theda and I started out with 40¢ rods from Montgomery Ward,
and we fished with worms, not flies. We rubbed neat's foot
oil into our hiking boots in a vain attempt to make them wa-
terproof so that when we waded into the cold streams we
wouldn't freeze. We froze! We had no rubber hip boots.
But even so we caught trout in the Rio Grande and Conejos
rivers and we usually cooked our trout right away at streamside. In case you don't know it, a freshly caught trout will
curl up in your skillet and is rather difficult to cook properly.
Only after it has lain around in your creel for several hours
will it lie flat in your skillet. Not knowing that trout like to
sleep late in the mornings (probably after a late night of

(Drawing by Anne Himmelberger-Caruso)

chasing insects), we usually started fishing before sunup, and cooked our trout for breakfast, along with bacon, fried potatoes and bread toasted over the coals. Oh, the good old days!

But our Alamosa friends frowned on our midwestern fishing habits and soon taught us fly fishing. By the time we left for Chicago in 1934 I was beginning to tie my own flies and I owned a cheap fly rod. Sometimes on Sunday mornings in our apartment, in sunless Chicago, I would get out my fly rod and pretend I was casting in the Conejos, and maybe tie up a few flies. I was thus able to fantasize myself out of my homesickness--sometimes.

After our return to Colorado in 1937 I went in for trout fishing in a big way, acquiring a Granger Special fly rod, rubber hip boots, and all kinds of fly tying feathers, furs, etc., from Herters. Theda joined me and became a better fly caster than I was, but unfortunately she gave up

the sport because I kept telling her how and where to fish.
My bossiness became a problem. I made the same mistake
with our two sons, and it wasn't until they got away from
home that they both became avid and skillful trout fishermen.
We now fish together comfortably.

The whole trout fishing milieu in Colorad has changed
completely since 1931. Although in the early days one had to
put up with Texans who drove their Cadillacs down the middle
of our mountain roads and who with their oil money bought up
many stream properties in southern Colorado and posted the
streams so we natives couldn't fish in them, there was still
plenty of open water in which to fish. Today, many of Colorado's best fishing waters are owned by wealthy individuals
and clubs and are closed to the public, for example the
stretch of water between Meeker and Trapper's Lake. Thanks
to the efforts of the State Game and Fish Department, and to
organizations like Trout Unlimited and the Sierra Club, some
open water still exists, but the best waters are privately
owned.

And, to make matters worse, many of our best streams
have been dammed and turned into reservoirs. Thus, mobs
of slobs can now enjoy sitting in their boats on their fat bot-
toms, drinking beer and throwing the cans into the water, and
trolling for trout with cheese and marshmallow balls for bait.
This is called making our natural resources available to the
People. What it really is is stealing our water resources
so that the developers, the banks and wealthy promoters
(usually outsiders) can encourage unlimited population growth,
so that they can make a lot of money. In our frenzy to make
use of Colorado's shale and coal resources, our few remain-
ing streams will be dammed to provide water for the processing of shale and to cool the electrical plants that will be fired
with Colorado coal. If you want to peep into the future, fly
over the four corners area today and see the smoke coming
out of those massive plants. Our future looks pretty dismal.

There are still many good fishing waters on the western slope, but on the eastern side there are only two good
fishing streams left in the Denver and north area--a short
stretch of the South Platte west of Denver and the Cache de
Poudre west of Fort Collins. Boulder Creek, once a fine
trout stream, is now barren except for a demonstration area
on the east edge of Boulder--as reclaimed by the Boulder
chapter of Trout Unlimited.

As further evidence of the decline in quality, the trout season is now open the year around, which gives the slobs an excuse to harass the trout all winter with their marshmallow balls. In the olden days, when the season opened May 25th and closed the end of October, one could dream all winter about where one would go on opening day. Conversation began with the question, "Where are you opening this year?" We have lost the joy of anticipation, and that's a big loss.

There are two aspects of trout fishing that give great pleasure even when fishing itself is not involved. The first is collecting the feathers, furs and new synthetic materials now used in tying flies. For example, right now I am seeking a supply of eyebrows from Great Horned Owls to use as legs on my Black Drake Nymphs and as wings on my Rat Faced McDougalls. It is now illegal to shoot these owls, and dealers can't sell the feathers. So, if any of my readers happens to have a stuffed Great Horned Owl sitting, unused, in his or her attic, please clip off the eyebrows and send them to me, collect. A true fly tier must haunt the women's sewing and knit shops seeking new materials, such as a new yarn called "Dazzle-aire," which Polly Roseborough, an expert at tying nymphs, says can be bought at K-Marts. But I'm a bit shy about hanging around in the ladies' departments of these stores. I once came close to committing a crime in an elevator when I almost grabbed a lady's hat for the rare feathers it contained. I managed to suppress my urge, but just barely.

The second joy is reading about fishing and fly tying. I have a six-foot shelf of such books for nighttime reading, and each month at least one new book is published to tempt us. What causes this literary ouburst is that the angling journalists have discovered a golden market--thousands of daydreaming fisherpersons with visions of flies and trout in their eyes. The photography in the new books is terrific, and just think of all those new bugs that are being discovered.

A fly tier faces domestic risks. For example, show me a fly tier who dyes his own feathers and furs in his wife's kitchen, using her favorite pots and pans, and I'll show you a man who doesn't clear the hair out of the sinks and strainers, or the stains out of pans. Ideally, a dyer should have a room of his own equipped with a sink and stove. I am required to use my own set of pans and strainers, and woe unto me if I don't clean out the sink.

And then there is the problem of space. In my case, my angling gear is stored in a 12-drawer large Danish desk, in a three-drawer cabinet, in two plastic sewing boxes, and in parts of four clothes closets--not to mention the gear I keep in our mountain cabin. My excuse is that while I may have no financial estate to pass along to my sons, think of all the fishing tackle, including thousands of well tied flies, they will inherit!

My interest in trout fishing was in part responsible for our building our mountain cabin. In 1940, after my summer at the Faculty Ranch with President Norlin, both Theda and I saw the virtue of having a mountain cabin, especially if it could be located near good fishing water, as a retreat from the pressure of Boulder's busy pace. We and Professor Leslie Lewis, one of our fishing and poker friends, began searching for such land. We soon found just what we wanted on the southeast shoulder of the Twin Sisters Mountain, south of Estes Park, an hour's drive from Boulder. There was good stream fishing nearby and also hundreds of beaver ponds in the Cabin Creek drainage area.

Pooling our almost nonexistent financial resources, three families joined together and purchased a $2\frac{1}{2}$-acre plot at $75.00 per acre (it would now cost from $4,000-$5,000 per acre), and started our cabins. I built the first unit of ours, 10' by 20' with the help of a hammer, a saw and a wood chisel. Since there was no electricity there at that time, power tools would have been useless even if we could have afforded them. The lumber we used came from a nearby sawmill--a tree one day and boards being nailed up the next! The boards were full of sap, very heavy and impossible to saw straight. Nevertheless, the cabin was weather tight. The design Theda and I had worked out turned out well, and was quite appropriate to its setting. Since my only previous experience with construction came from helping my father build pig pens when I was young, I naturally had to solve building problems as they arose.

Later, as time went on and our needs increased, I added more units--the last two with the help of power tools and slightly cured lumber. Now we do have electricity but still no indoor water supply or plumbing--thus we avoid the problems of freezing pipes. We can use our cabin all winter, using roof snow and water for work water and carrying in our drinking water.

We cook on a beloved wood/coal stove, than which there is nothing that can do a better job of cooking a turkey in the oven, or of following a recipe that calls for quick and subtle changes of stove surface temperatures. Neither a gas nor an electric range equals its capabilities.

We heat our cabin with a large Franklin fireplace stove, supplemented, in our old age, with a wall propane furnace for early mornings. Although there is a small well-insulated room housing a portable shower and a chemical toilet for night use, we mostly use an outdoor privy, so placed that the view from the open door looks to the face of Meeker Peak--a view that is wonderfully calming to the soul and the bowel.

During the fourteen years we lived in Iowa we spent most of our summers living in the cabin, simply and peacefully. Our two sons, Peter and David, learned to play together there and to love the mountains and the simple kind of living that the cabin permitted. Now in their thirties, each boy lives in a mountain cabin, one in Colorado and one in Wyoming. Peter once explained to one of our guests who wanted to know what we did all summer, that "at the cabin you don't do, you be." Much of the writing that I have done has been done, in the first draft at least, at the cabin. The mood is just right for writing.

Many of our professional and personal friends have visited us there and they too have fallen under the cabin's spell. All of the furniture is hand made, each piece carefully and modestly designed for its purpose. One of our two davenports (made of aspen poles and boards) is especially rich in tradition, in that two of our visiting friends claim that their first-born child was conceived on the davenport. I never told them that the reason probably was that the mattress was unusually firm, and that to sleep there bathed in moonbeans while watching the fire in the Franklin stove die down would take the tenseness out of anybody.

Even though our house in Boulder is a wonderfully comfortable and romantic place to live, with a small but noisy creek flowing by it within six feet, our hearts always leap up when we get to the cabin, and so it is with our children, our granddaughter and our friends.

CONCLUSION

How does one wind up an autobiography at age seventy-one, when, so to speak, one isn't ready to leave the stage?

I could try to pass along some words of wisdom for the next generation of librarians, but the trouble is that I don't have any special words of wisdom to pass along. I don't know what the libraries of the future will be like, except that they will retain some of the qualities of the present ones. As long as one keeps straight in his head the differences between the carriers of information and the information itself, I don't see how the electronic revolution can be harmful to libraries. Whatever people put into their minds has got to go in through their ears or eyes, and presumably whatever medium we use to get it in ought to be the most appropriate one available. And since it should be obvious that people differ in the capacities of their minds, the speed with which they can learn, and the kinds of things they want in their minds, as well as in the ways in which they like to put things in, I see no lack of opportunity for all the media to be useful. If we can sort of relax and let the information flow where it will (remembering always that man doesn't live by information alone), it will be easier for us to organize and manage the carriers than it will be if we concentrate our thinking on the way we "need to do it."

Personally, I have a hard time getting complex ideas and thoughts into my head (no doubt due to my limited intelligence) and I'll use whatever means there are to get the stuff in. I do know that I sometimes have to go over and over a difficult idea before I can understand it, and woe be to the medium that won't let me do the necessary viewing-- as one can when reading a book, or as one can't when watching a TV documentary. I'm thinking how frustrated I was recently while watching Pete Ustinov's interpretation of Einstein, because I needed to have several scenes repeated--an impossibility.

Or, I could write about achieving happiness--not the

major ways all mankind has found to achieve happiness, but
the little, special, unique ways I have invented in finding it.
I could mention one or two: I find it nice to tie my own
trout flies and then to persuade trout to strike them. I find
it pleasant to take out my frustrations arising from working
with stupid people by saying, "Off with your head, A____
B____," as I identify with the block of wood I split for my
Franklin fireplace. I like to eat popcorn when I'm reading
for fun or when I watch an exciting game on TV. I like to
go into a shop in Mexico and say something that will evoke
from the female clerks those flashing smiles that one almost
never sees in the more sophisticated countries, or among
the light-skinned peoples of the world. And so on.

Or I could share my sense of wonderment at the stupidity of mankind. Why, for example, do we go on fighting
over religions when it is obvious that they all have the same
objective: to keep us from being frightened by our existence,
and when there is no evidence that one religion is any better
than the others at this task? Or, why can't we see that we
must develop a true world government that will have the authority and means to make us stop fighting one another? Or,
why can't we see that all peoples of the world are equally
capable when they have equal opportunity over a period of
time? Or why can't we Americans understand that political
conservatives are not true conservatives, and that what they
offer as doctrine is evil, not, as they say, an alternative?

Or, why don't we civilized people post on our ban-
ners, in spite of the fact that Karl Marx coined it, that
dynamite-laden slogan, "From each according to his ability,
to each according to his need?" It expresses dramatically
and exactly what civilization should be all about. Jesus
never said it so well. And the Soviets never really practiced it. It's available for our use.

Or, I could recall all the fine and generous things
people have done for me and my family. Or the wonderful
skill one surgeon has shown in saving the lives of two members of my family.

Or, I could talk about how luck played such a large
part in my life--luck in selecting the finest colleges and uni-
versities in which to study: Oberlin, Chicago and Western
Reserve. Luck in finding a wonderful wife. Luck in the way
I got my first jobs at Adams State and the University of
Colorado.

Or I could simply decide it's time to stop writing. And if anything especially interesting happens in the future I can probably find ways of telling about it--if it's worth telling.

REFERENCES CITED

Bauman, C. H. The Influence of Angus Snead Macdonald and the Snead Bookstack on Library Architecture. Metuchen, N. J. Scarecrow Press, 1972.

Brown, H. Faulkner, editor. Planning the Academic Library: Metcalf and Ellsworth at York. Newcastle upon Tyne, England: Oriel Press, 1971.

Burchard, J., J. Boyd, and C. David. Planning University Buildings. Princeton, N. J.: Princeton University Press, 1949.

Commager, H. S. Living Ideas in America. New York: Harper, 1951.

Cooperative Committee on Large University Library Building Planning. Minutes. Various.

Dix, William. "Centralized Cataloging and University Libraries, Title II." Library Trends, 1967, pp. 98-101.

Ellsworth, R. E. Academic Library Buildings: Issues and Solutions. Boulder, Colorado: The Colorado Associated Academic Press, 1973.

_____. "The A. L. A.'s Anniversary: An Appraisal." Library Journal 78: 547-550, April 1, 1963, p. 549.

_____. "Another Chance for Centralized Cataloging." The Colorado Academic Librarian, Vol. 1, no. 1, Fall, 1963.

_____. Buildings. The State of the Art Series. Vol. 3, Part 1. Metuchen, N. J.: Scarecrow Press, 1960.

_____. "Centralized Cataloging for Scholarly Libraries." Library Quarterly, 15: 237-240, July 1945.

_____. "Critique of Library Associations." Library Quarterly, 4: 382-400, Oct. 1961.

_____. The Economics of Book Storage in College and University Libraries. Metuchen, N. J. : Scarecrow Press, 1969.

_____. "Libraries, Students and Faculty." The Cornell Library Conference. Ithaca: Cornell University Library, 1964. Pp. 67 and 75.

_____. Planning the College and University Library Building. Boulder, Colorado: Pruett Press, 1960. Second edition, 1968.

_____. Planning Manual for Academic Library Buildings. Metuchen, N. J. : Scarecrow Press, 1973.

_____. The School Library. The Library of Education Series. New York: Center for Applied Research in Education, Inc. , 1965.

_____ and Sarah M. Harris. The American Right Wing: A Report to the Fund for the Republic. Urbana: University of Illinois, Graduate Library School. Occasional Papers, No. 59, 1960.

_____ and Hobart D. Wagener. The School Library: Facilities for Independent Study in the Secondary School. New York: Educational Facilities Laboratories, Inc. , 1963.

Garza Mercado, Ario. Funcion y Forma de la Biblioteca Universitaria. Journadas 83. Mexico: El Colegio de Mexico, 1977.

Johnson, Gerald W. "A Challenge to Americans," Look, July 31, 1951.

_____. This American People. New York: Harper, 1951.

Kilpatrick, N. and R. E. Ellsworth. "The Midwest Reaches for the Stars." College and Research Libraries. April, 1948, pp. 1-9.

Kirk, Russell. Editorial in the National Review, Nov. 20, 1962, p. 393.

Millett, John. The Academic Community. New York, McGraw-Hill: 1962.

Margolis, Howard. "Right Wingers Seem to Be Almost Everywhere: Notes on a Report to the Fund for the Republic." Science, 134: 2025-27, Dec. 22, 1961.

Swisher, D. and C. Richards. Selective Trout. New York: Crown, 1971.

INDEX

Academic Library Buildings: Architectural Issues
    & Solutions 114
The ACRL & the federation plan for ALA
    reorganization 128ff.
Adams State College 1
Al Mani, Dr. (Riyadh University) 99
Al Nafi, Dr. 101
Allen, Steve 76
American Association of University Professors 133
American Library Association, comments on 123ff.;
    137: 75th Anniversary Celebration 78
American Right Wing project 74
Association of Research Libraries. Comments on 129ff.;
    Iowa City meeting 59; Shared Cataloging Committee
    73; University Microfilms Inc.--Committee on Pub-
    lishing Dissertations 123
Athens, Greece airport bombing incident 95

Barker, Victoria Siegfried 40
Bauman, Charles 55
Bay, John Christian 31
Bean, Donald E. 49
Boyd, Julian 56, 57
Brahm, Walter 27
British Lending Library 92
Bromley, James 76
Brown, H. Faulkner vii, 87
Brown, University Library 43
Buck, Paul 65, 138
Burchard, John 56, 83
Burrows Bros. Book Store, Cleveland 26
Butler, Pierce 31, 34

Cabell, Leo 86
Cambridge (England) University Library 91
Carnovsky, Leon 33

Center for Research Libraries   see   Midwest Inter-
    Library Center
Centralized Cataloging   61ff.
Clapp, Werner   66
Clift, David   80
Colorado Academic Central Processing Center   135
Colorado Academic Libraries--editorial   65ff.
Colorado Library Association--President 1936,
    1937 & 1958   123
Colorado State Teachers College   37, 41
Commager, Henry   78
Consulting work--comments on   115ff.
Cooperative Committee on Large University
    Library Building Planning   56ff.
Cornell University Library Dedication   136
Cory, John   79, 127
Council on Library Resources   114
Cowles, Gardner   78
Cronin, John   60, 73, 130

David, Charles   51, 57
Dawson, John   70
Desert party in Saudi Arabia   101
Desmets, Claudine   98
Dissertation--writing   37
Dissertations Abstracts project   58ff.
Dix, William S.   70ff.
Doany, Atallah   99
Dougherty, Richard   136

Early years in Iowa   16ff.
Educational Facilities Laboratories, Inc.   86, 88, 114, 124
Edwards, Wesley   101
El Colegio de Mexico Library   110ff.
Ellsworth, Clayton, brother   23
Ellsworth, John David, son   43
Ellsworth, Peter Chapman, son   43
Ellsworth, Theda, wife   everywhere
Eshelman, William   119
Esterquest, Ralph   55, 133
Evans, Luther   64

Fellini, William   104
Ferguson, William   126

Flanders, Senator   79
Fleming, Thomas   27
Fletcher, Scott   79
Ford Foundation   79, 99, 110, 118
Fund for the Republic   75
Funari, John   118
Fussler, Herman   124

Garza Mercado, Ario   100ff.
General Federation of Women's Clubs   78
Gerber, John   133
Gottschalk, G. R.   134
Graduate Library School   see   University of Chicago.
    Graduate Library School
Graham, Skip   79

Harris, Sarah   see   The American Right Wing project
Heald, Henry   132
Heritage Library--University of Iowa   48
High school years   21, 22
Howe, Harriett, E.   9
Hug, Mr. (Riyadh University)   99
Human Relations Area Files, Inc.   122, 131

Ifield (England) Lower School   90
Ingraham, Mark   132

Jackson, W. Carl   86
Jesse, William   87
Joeckel, Carlton   33
Johnson, Gerald   78

Kampf, Louise   7
Kaplan, Louis   70
Khomeini, A.   98
Kilgour, Frederick   124
Kilpatrick, Norman   64
King, Jonathan   88
Kirk, Russell   77
KKK in Colorado   45
Klauder, C. Z.   41

Lake District, England 88
Lancour, Harold 75
Laves, Walter 79
Law Library Association--Governance controversy 129
Lester, Robert 124ff.
Libraries, future of 150
Library associations, my relations with 122ff.
Liebaers, Herman 95
Logsdon, Richard 71ff.
Lord, Milton 137
Low, Edmund 73
Luckman, Charles 119

Macdonald, Angus Snead 41
McDiarmid, E. W. 51ff. , 83
Maier, Joan 136
Margolis, Howard 76
Marriage, my 29
Mead, Margaret 79
Merritt, Leroy 62
Metcalf, K. D. 87, 120, 138
Mexican hospitality 112
Mexico. Autonema Metropolitana Universidad.
   Iztapolapa Library 113; Department of
   Horticulture library 113; Institute for
   Electrical Researches library 113
Middlebrook, Vice President 133
Midwest Inter Library Center 51ff. , 132
Milam, Carl 43, 122, 125, 127
Milczewski, Marion 92
Miller, Robert 80
Millett, John 137
Modular planning--origins 41ff. , 47ff.
Mount St. Scholistica (Kansas) library 121

Newton, Quigg 85
Norlin, George 41, 44ff.

Oberlin College library 24: Library project
   120ff. ; years 23ff.
O'Conner, L. C. 58
Ogburn, W. F. 32
Ohio College Library Center 73
Orne, Jerrold 136
Oxford (England) University Law Library 114

Pahlavi Imperial Library, Iran   95ff.
Piasecki, Wladyslaw   30
Peter--son   43
Pittsburgh University Consultation   117
Plough, The (pub in Ifield)   90
Poker with President Truman, almost   141
Porter, Lois   75
Powell, Benjamin & Betsy   80
Power, Eugene   59ff.
Public Affairs Press   76
Purdy, G. Flint   36, 38, 80

Randall, W.   34
Rice, Stevens   60
Rice University library   57
Right Wing project   74ff.
Riyadh (Saudi Arabia) University library project   98ff.
RLIN   73
Robinson, A. L.   117
Rose & Crown Pub   92
Russell, John Dale   134

Sabbatical year, 1969-1970   114ff.
San Luis Valley, Colorado   3
Saudi Arabia, comments on   102ff.
Schnapper, Geo.   75
The School Library (E. F. L.) book   89
Schwegmann, George   65
SCONL   92
Selden, W. K. , as Exec. Dir. of the National
    Commission on Accreditation   129
Seminars on Library building planning   86, 87
Seth, Jon   93
Sex among farm animals   14, 15
Shafa, Dr. S.   96
Sharify, Nasser   98
Shaw, Ralph   91
Shorey, Paul   30
Simon Bolivar University, Venezuela   104ff.
Skiing in Colorado--early   142
Skipper, James   67, 72
Smith, C. H.   9, 39
Stevenson, Grace   79
Stockholm University Library project   93ff.
Stout, Ruth   75

Strong, George Franklin 9, 27, 29
Subject divisional plan at Colorado 42, 45ff.
Swank, Raynard 40, 41

Thompson, Anthony 91
Thompson, C. S. 1, 29, 31
Tingle, Vern & Edna 6
Tippo, Oswald 83
Titograd University (Yugoslavia) Library 106ff.
Trout fishing 45, 142ff.
Truman, President Harry 141
Tyler, Ralph W. 134

U. S. News & World Report 77
UNESCO 106
University Microfilms Inc. 59ff.
University of Chicago. Graduate Library
    School vii, 29, 30, 32-40
University of Colorado--library director of 40, 47ff. , 83
University of Iowa--library director of 47ff. , 83
Urquhart, Donald 92
Ustinov, Peter 150

Vosper, Robert 92

Wagener, Hobart 89
Wahaibi, Professor (Riyadh University) 100
Waples, Douglas 1, 29-31, 34ff. , 37, 38
Warner, Lloyd 32, 38
Weinstock, Ruth 89
Wells College Library consultation 119
Welsh, William 130
Western Reserve University Library staff 29
Wheeler, Joseph B. 41
Wildermuth, Judge 133
Williams, Gordon 66, 133
Williamson, C. S. 31
Wilson, Eugene H. 80, 83
Wilson, John 78
Wilson, L. R. 35ff.
Wirth, Louis 32, 38
Works, George 38
Wyer, Malcolm 43

Wyoming University library consultation 118

York (England) School of Applied Architecture 87

Zaher, Mrs. C. R. 106